Mediterranean Diet Air Fryer Cookbook for Beginners

Easy, Delicious & Healthy Mediterranean Diet Recipes to Heal Your Body & Help You Lose Weight (30-Day Meal Plan to Kickstart Your Healthy Lifestyle)

Barbon Joner

Table of contents

Introduction 6

Chapter 1: Understanding the Mediterranean Diet? 7

    What Is the Mediterranean Diet? 7

    Benefits of the Mediterranean Diet 7

    How Do I Start a Mediterranean Diet? 8

Chapter 2: The Basics of Air Fryer 9

    What is an Air Fryer? 9

    Advantages of Using an Air Fryer 9

    How to Start Cooking in An Air Fryer? 10

    How to Clean and Maintain Your Air Fryer 11

Chapter 3: Foods to Eat 13

Chapter 4: Foods to Avoid 15

Chapter 5: 30-Day Meal Plan 16

Chapter 6: Breakfast and Brunch 19

    Fried Guacamole 19

    German Pancakes 21

    Tofu Scramble 22

    Breakfast Biscuits 24

    French Toast Sticks 25

    Frittata 26

    Breakfast Bombs 28

    Bacon with Eggs 30

    Omelet 31

    Hash Browns 32

Chapter 7: Poultry 34

    Mediterranean Breaded Chicken 34

    Chicken Drumstick 35

    Chicken Breast 37

    Thai Chili Fried Chicken Wings 38

    Buffalo Chicken Wings 40

    Chicken Fajita Rollups 41

    Tso's Chicken 43

Lemon Pepper Chicken 45

Caribbean Spiced Chicken 46

Fennel Chicken 47

Chapter 8: Appetizers and Siders 49

Patatas Bravas 49

Cauliflower 51

Onion Rings 52

Spicy Chicken Thighs 53

Zucchini, Yellow Squash, and Carrots 55

Mac and Cheese 56

Whole-Wheat Pizzas 57

Chicken Nuggets 58

Sweet Potato Cauliflower Patties 59

Cauliflower Rice 61

Chapter 9: Beef, Pork, and Lamb 63

Meatloaf Sliders 63

Scotch Eggs 65

Steak Nuggets 66

Beef and Mushroom Patties 68

Italian-Style Meatballs 69

Rib Eye Steak 71

Steak Bites and Mushrooms 72

Pork Chops 73

Pork Dumplings with Dipping Sauce 74

Spicy Bacon Bites 76

Spicy Lamb Steak 77

Herbed Lamb Chops 78

Chapter 10: Vegetarian 79

Brussels Sprouts 79

Roasted Rainbow Vegetables 80

Falafel 81

Green Beans with Bacon 83

Parmesan Brussel Sprouts 84

Ginger Soy Tofu 85

Loaded Potatoes 87
Veggie Quesadillas 88
Chapter 11: Fish and Seafood 90
Tomato Basil Scallops 90
Fish Sticks 92
Salmon Patties 93
Shrimp Scampi 94
Garlic Lime Shrimp 95
Parmesan Shrimp 96
Salmon and Asparagus 97
Catfish with Green Beans 98
Chapter 12: Dessert 100
Apple Chips 100
Churros 101
Fruit Crumble Mug Cakes 103
Banana Bread 104
Cheesecake Bites 106
Spiced Apples 107
Key Lime Cupcakes 108
Grilled Pineapple 109
Conclusion 110

Introduction

Fried foods are the biggest contributors to hypertension, high blood pressure and heart attacks, and eventually death. Obviously, fried foods are simple carbs with lots of saturated fats. These fried foods will not let you maintain your health and push further away from fitness goals.

Now, it's time to incorporate air fryer in your lifestyle. With an air fryer, you can cut down macronutrients, saturated fats, and calories by more than sixty percent. Along with air fryer, the Mediterranean diet will tremendously help you get back on the track. And unlike other diet plans, this diet doesn't come with restrictions or eliminations, and that's why it is easy to adopt and follow without missing out all the tasty foods and flavors.

And the best part – you can easily share meals and enjoy life with more comfort and fewer efforts.

With the 30-days meal plan and scrumptious Mediterranean diet recipes in this cookbook, the air fryer will become your favorite new kitchen tool. Just imagine the meals you can make with the air fryer.

Read on to know more.

Chapter 1: Understanding the Mediterranean Diet?

What Is the Mediterranean Diet?

The Mediterranean Sea is the sea that is fully bordered by landmass, the northern border formed by the southern European countries such as Turkey and Greece, and the southern border by the African countries like Egypt. The different countries' traditions, cuisines, and products have been thoroughly blended, giving rise to a unique culture that is also shown in their food. The diet of the inhabitants living in this unique culture is known as the Mediterranean diet.

This diet was made famous by research that was held in 1970 to study coronary heart disease. It showed that the people living in these regions have a low risk of developing heart diseases compared to other parts of the world. Thus, its importance was heightened across the globe. The diet mainly consists of different varieties of vegetables, fruits, beans, legumes, nuts, and oils. There is also an abundance of seafood in their cuisines. The diet consists of a significant amount of fats which is provided by the white meat and olive oil. Unlike the oils produced by animal fat, these oils contain healthy fat, which helps to lower body cholesterol and keep the body healthy.

Many of their traditional dishes are not only popular for their health benefits but also are known delicacies with their rich amount of fresh vegetables and fruits, and a variety of sea flavors. Dishes as Prosciutto shows great use of grains, while Tabbouleh's main ingredients are vegetables.

Benefits of the Mediterranean Diet

The advantages provided by the diet are not limited to, providing just a delicious meal. The extensive research done in the last 50 years showed that this diet had been linked to improving the lives of natives of these regions by safeguarding them from an array of diseases. It is the main reason why the Mediterranean diet has been trending. Multiple people from different backgrounds belong in this area, and the food brings all those different people together.

There are many ways that the diet increases the mortality of human life. The oils present in the dishes driven from white meat and plants lowers LDL content, which is linked to heart diseases and blood pressure. Herbs are used in high quantity which has different medicinal properties. The diet because of the low use of sugar and sugary substitutes it has reduces the chances of diabetes and glucose levels remains controlled. It also improves vision and brain function due to increased uptake of vegetables and fruits, which provides adequate levels of vitamins and minerals. Due to improved brain function, the chances of developing Alzheimer's disease is low. Eating fresh ingredients also reduces the probability of cancer development. It also lowers the risk of developing rheumatoid arthritis and bone disorders.

The western world has been gripped with obesity and its associated diseases. The diet also helps people to reduce their appetite and lose weight. This may be the main reason why the inhabitants of Mediterranean regions are healthier compared to other western countries such as the US.

How Do I Start a Mediterranean Diet?

Mediterranean diet can be accomplished by anyone. It doesn't put stress over your body or your mind but on the contrary, rejuvenates it. Unlike other diet practices, eating only a few ingredients will not be enough. A vast array of vegetables, fruits, and other products are a part of this diet.

Eating Plans

First, the diet consists of many types of oils, and these can be sourced from mainly olive oil. Therefore, replace all animal made oil products mainly with olive oil. Fish and other seafood are also a good source of fat. They are rich in Omega 3 fats, which is very healthy for the body.

Secondly, cut down red meat as much as possible. It can be consumed in low amounts, but mainly the protein consumed is in the form of seafood, grains, and beans. Red meat can be taken in the form of lamb, chicken, and turkey. Eggs and dairy products can also be used.

Thirdly, drink a good amount of water each day. Water is overlooked in many diets, but for a good lifestyle, water intake is essential. Replace all your beverages with water. It is important to hydrate yourself whenever thirsty.

Lifestyle

Lastly and most important is the fact that the diet also requires the Individual to follow a healthy routine. Sleep should not be compromised. Sleep is vital in maintaining a healthy body and brain function. Adequate sleep and completing one's sleep cycle should be a routine. Exercises are done daily. By doing daily physical activities, one's weight will be controlled, and the entire body will benefit and become stronger in the process. Most diets don't discuss the effect of the mind on the body. Stresses on the mind should be kept to a minimum. All this together will not only increase your health but also your brain.

Chapter 2: The Basics of Air Fryer

What is an Air Fryer?

With technology giving birth to different and unique inventions every day to satisfy the hunger of innovation in society, the modernization of the everyday kitchen is also seen. As time passes by, many new machines are introduced into the daily life of a common man. Among the many devices that have made life more comfortable with their usefulness and design, the Air Fryer is also an excellent tool which has many benefits.

An Air Fryer is a device that cooks food not by using oil but by heated air with no compromise on the texture and flavor of the dish. The Air Fryer is not only used for frying up food but can also be used for many other tasks such as grilling or baking. It ensures that the food is cooked evenly and thoroughly. Its design is such that it fits in a compact area and works via electricity.

It has many different parts:

1. The frying basket: it is a stainless steel basket in which the food is placed for cooking. This can be replaced by any other utensils, such as a pizza pan.
2. The timer: the timer is set accordingly; a red light indicates when the time has been finished.
3. The temperature controller: The temperature of the Air Fryer has a high range from 175 to 400F. Adjust the temp knob to achieve the desired temperature.
4. The air inlet/outlet: It is used to release the hot air and steam arising during the cooking process from the back of the device. It is, therefore, important that the device remains kept in a spacious area.

Advantages of Using an Air Fryer

With the demand rising of fat-free and healthy food, air fried food has also become a hot topic. With innovation striving to make every day more efficient, the air fryer has many benefits to improve daily lives. It has many advantages:

- Multi-purpose

It is not only a fryer but also a griller, a baker, or a pizza maker. Instead of purchasing tens of different devices, one can only buy an air fryer to fulfill the many requirements of one's kitchen.

- Healthier Food

With the use of hot air instead of oil to cook the food, the food cooked has a significant reduction in oil and fat content. Fat is related to increasing the risk of many diseases, such as heart disease, hypertension, and obesity. It does all this without hindering the flavors of the food being cooked. Because the fryer evenly distributes heat, the air fried food is as crispy as oil fried.

- Reduces Time consumption

Air fryer is set for a given time and cooks food at the provided temperature thoroughly. Usually, to get healthy cooked food, one must slave over a hot stove for some time but because of the air fryer, time can be saved.

- Reduces Injury

There are a lot of accidents involving the kitchen, either someone's finger is burned, or hot oil is splattered all over. The air fryer does not require oil or an open flame, so many injuries linked with it are not a worry.

- Reheating

Leftover food to be reheated can be easily done with the help of an air fryer. Usually, reheating food takes a lot of effort and time, but the air fryer does this job very efficiently.

- Easy to Use

Cooking is a complicated process requiring a lot of skills, but the air fryer makes cooking very easy. The ingredients need only to be put into the machine, and buttons need to be pushed. Anyone, even someone with no prior experience with cooking, can make great meals.

How to Start Cooking in An Air Fryer?

Firstly, the Air Fryer must be in a spacious place to allow heat to escape and prevent damage to its parts. It should be put on top of a heat resistance surface.

Secondly, pull out the frying basket gently from the machine. It is recommended to preheat the device for 5 minutes before using it. Simply set the desired temperature for 5 mins and then after the time is completed, pull out the basket.

Now place the food inside the container. Not more than ⅔ of the container should be filled. If required, the container can be greased with an oil spray to avoid sticking of the food. If fatty foods are placed, add a little bit of water so that the container remains clean.

Now place the container gently inside and close the lid. The electric cord should be connected, and the time and temperature should be set. Both indicators should be on until the frying is completed.

The food can be stirred flipped or shaken as per requirement.

For grilling, the food must be flipped at regular intervals until it gets a good color on both sides.

When finished, a sound will go off. Push the off button just once, then wait for 30 seconds for the device to completely turn off.

When done, serve the food in a serving dish and leave the basket out of the device for some time before putting it back in.

How to Clean and Maintain Your Air Fryer

Maintaining the Air Fryer

- When buying the Air Fryer, quality needs to be addressed before anything else. Don't give in to or purchase an Air Fryer on the bases of reviews or price. It should be bought from an established, and authentic source.
- Don't overfill the device; the fryer basket needs space. If it is overloaded, the food will not be properly cooked, and the taste and texture will be affected.
- Don't place the Air Fryer just anywhere. It needs to be placed in an area that will allow some space. It should always be put on top of a heat resistance surface
- Don't put the basket back in the Fryer without it cooling it down first. It should be cleaned and cool when reinserted.
- Don't follow the instructions of temperature or time given on packages or recipes for ovens or microwaves. Air Fryer is its device, which requires the settings to be adjusted.

Cleaning of the Air Fryer

The air fryer needs to be cleaned every month. If it is left without cleaning, it will start to give off a smell. If some food pieces are stuck in the heating outlet, black smoke will start to come out of the device when turned on.

When cleaning the device, it is important to keep in mind that no corrosive or strong chemicals should be used in cleaning. Also, hard and abrasive brushes are to be avoided. They can cause damage to the stainless steel of the basket, which will be irreversible.

Before cleaning the equipment, the device should be turned off and left to completely cooled down. Unplug the device and neatly place the cord to avoid hindrance.

Firstly, the basket needs to be clean thoroughly. Due to use, the basket will accumulate grease over it, and it will be difficult to remove. Use water and dishwashing liquid to clean the surface of the basket. If the stains are not easily removed, then leave the basket filled with water and dishwashing liquid for a certain amount of time. Then with a sponge clean the basket.

After washing, the basket needs to be rubbed and dried by a kitchen towel. Once thoroughly dried, the basket should be reinserted.

Chapter 3: Foods to Eat

Here's is what you can eat and add in your meals for the Mediterranean diet

Protein

Chicken, turkey, lamb, fish, seafood, and vegan alternates like tofu, tempeh, and seitan

Fats and Oil

Olive oil, coconut oil, avocado oil, grass-fed butter

Vegetables

All vegetables such as red onion, tomatoes, broccoli, cauliflower, Brussel sprouts, zucchini, bell peppers, artichokes, cucumber, eggplant, olives, potatoes, sweet potatoes, turnip, yams, greens like kale, spinach, collard, arugula, and all root vegetables

Fruits

All fruits like peach, apricot, apple, grapes, pear, watermelon, dates, cherries, all berries like blackberries, raspberries, strawberries, and blueberries

Nuts and Seeds

Walnuts, almonds, hazelnuts, peanuts, pistachios, cashews, and all unsweetened nuts

Grains

Beans, lentils, chickpeas, whole grains, steel-cut and old-fashioned oatmeal, quinoa, wheat, bulgur, farro, couscous, corn, brown rice, buckwheat, whole-wheat pasta, whole-grain crackers, all-bran cereals

Dairy

Eggs, yogurt, low-fat cheeses, low-fat milk, buttermilk, feta cheese, Brie cheese, and goat cheese

Sweeteners

Erythritol, swerve sweetener, stevia, honey

Sauces and Condiments

No-sugar tomato sauce, pesto, apple cider vinegar, balsamic vinegar, low-sodium soy sauce, tahini sauce, aioli, unsweetened BBQ sauce, unsweetened tomato ketchup, organic teriyaki sauce, hummus

Drinks

Unsweetened, tea, unsweetened coffee, water, red wine

Herbs and Spices

All organic herbs and spices

Chapter 4: Foods to Avoid

Skip the following foods on the Mediterranean diet

Protein

Red meat such as of beef and pork, bacon, processed meat

Fats and Oil

Trans fat, margarine, high-fat butter

Nuts and Seeds

Nut butters, sugar-coated nuts

Grains

Sugar-sweetened cereals, ready-made waffles, pancakes, crackers, snack foods

Dairy

Ice cream, sweetened yogurt, processed cheeses

Sweeteners

White sugar

Drinks

Processed fruit juices, sweetened coffee, sweetened tea, soda

Chapter 5: 30-Day Meal Plan

Day 1

Breakfast: German Pancakes

Lunch: Buffalo Chicken Wings

Dinner: Catfish With Green Beans

Dessert: Key Lime Cupcakes

Day 2

Breakfast: German Pancakes

Lunch: Buffalo Chicken Wings

Dinner: Catfish With Green Beans

Dessert: Key Lime Cupcakes

Day 3

Breakfast: German Pancakes

Lunch: Onion Rings

Dinner: Chicken Fajita Rollups

Dessert: Apple Chips

Day 4

Breakfast: German Pancakes

Lunch: Spicy Bacon Bites

Dinner: Cauliflower Rice

Dessert: Apple Chips

Day 5

Breakfast: Bacon with Eggs

Lunch: Brussels Sprouts

Dinner: Beef and Mushroom Patties

Dessert: Cheesecake Bites

Day 6

Breakfast: Bacon with Eggs

Lunch: Garlic Lime Shrimp

Dinner: Beef and Mushroom Patties

Dessert: Cheesecake Bites

Day 7

Breakfast: Frittata

Lunch: Chicken Drumstick

Dinner: Roasted Rainbow Vegetables

Dessert: Cheesecake Bites

Day 8

Breakfast: Frittata

Lunch: Spicy Lamb Steak

Dinner: Salmon Patties

Dessert: Grilled Pineapple

Day 9

Breakfast: Frittata

Lunch: Zucchini, Yellow Squash, and Carrots

Dinner: Salmon Patties

Dessert: Grilled Pineapple

Day 10

Breakfast: Frittata

Lunch: Steak Nuggets

Dinner: Lemon Pepper Chicken

Dessert: Churros

Day 11

Breakfast: Fried Guacamole

Lunch: Steak Nuggets

Dinner: Lemon Pepper Chicken

Dessert: Churros

Day 12

Breakfast: Fried Guacamole

Lunch: Green Beans with Bacon

Dinner: Italian-Style Meatballs

Dessert: Churros

Day 13

Breakfast: Hash Browns

Lunch: Scotch Eggs

Dinner: Italian-Style Meatballs

Dessert: Spiced Apples

Day 14

Breakfast: Hash Browns

Lunch: Green Beans with Bacon

Dinner: Ginger Soy Tofu

Dessert: Spiced Apples

Day 15

Breakfast: Hash Browns

Lunch: Fish Sticks

Dinner: Ginger Soy Tofu

Dessert: Banana Bread

Day 16

Breakfast: Hash Browns

Lunch: Fish Sticks

Dinner: Shrimp Scampi

Dessert: Banana Bread

Day 17

Breakfast: Breakfast Biscuits

Lunch: Thai Chili Fried Chicken Wings

Dinner: Shrimp Scampi

Dessert: Banana Bread

Day 18

Breakfast: Breakfast Biscuits

Lunch: Thai Chili Fried Chicken Wings

Dinner: Caribbean Spiced Chicken

Dessert: Banana Bread

Day 19

Breakfast: Breakfast Biscuits

Lunch: Sweet Potato Cauliflower Patties

Dinner: Caribbean Spiced Chicken

Dessert: Fruit Crumble Mug Cakes

Day 20

Breakfast: Breakfast Biscuits

Lunch: Sweet Potato Cauliflower Patties

Dinner: Meatloaf Sliders

Dessert: Fruit Crumble Mug Cakes

Day 21

Breakfast: Tofu Scramble

Lunch: Steak Bites and Mushrooms

Dinner: Veggie Quesadillas

Dessert: Fruit Crumble Mug Cakes

Day 22

Breakfast: Tofu Scramble

Lunch: Steak Bites and Mushrooms

Dinner: Tomato Basil Scallops

Dessert: Fruit Crumble Mug Cakes

Day 23

Breakfast: French Toast Sticks

Lunch: Loaded Potatoes

Dinner: Mediterranean Breaded Chicken

Dessert: Apple Chips

Day 24

Breakfast: French Toast Sticks

Lunch: Salmon and Asparagus

Dinner: Rib Eye Steak

Dessert: Apple Chips

Day 25

Breakfast: French Toast Sticks

Lunch: Salmon and Asparagus

Dinner: Parmesan Shrimp

Dessert: Key Lime Cupcakes

Day 26

Breakfast: French Toast Sticks

Lunch: Chicken Breast

Dinner: Fennel Chicken

Dessert: Key Lime Cupcakes

Day 27

Breakfast: Breakfast Bombs

Lunch: Mac and Cheese

Dinner: Pork Dumplings with Dipping Sauce

Dessert: Grilled Pineapple

Day 28

Breakfast: Breakfast Bombs

Lunch: Whole-Wheat Pizzas

Dinner: Herbed Lamb Chops

Dessert: Grilled Pineapple

Day 29

Breakfast: Omelet

Lunch: Falafel

Dinner: Herbed Lamb Chops

Dessert: Banana Bread

Day 30

Breakfast: Omelet

Lunch: Pork Chops

Dinner: Tso's Chicken

Dessert: Banana Bread

Chapter 6: Breakfast and Brunch

Fried Guacamole

Preparation time: 6 hours and 15 minutes
Cooking time: 16 minutes
Servings: 10

Ingredients:

- 1/3 cup almond flour
- 1 egg
- 1 1/2 cups panko bread crumbs
- 1 egg white

For Guacamole:

- 3 medium avocados, halved, pitted, peeled
- 1/3 cup chopped cilantro
- 1/3 cup chopped red onion
- ½ teaspoon ground black pepper
- 2 teaspoons ground cumin
- 1 teaspoon of sea salt
- 8 tablespoons almond flour
- 1 lime, juiced

Method:

1. Prepare guacamole and for this, take a bowl, add all its ingredients in it except for flour and mash with a fork until well combined.
2. Gradually mix the flour until thick and brownie dough-like batter comes together and freeze for 1 to 2 hours until the mixture has hardened.
3. Meanwhile, take a baking sheet, and then line it with aluminum foil.
4. After 2 hours, use a spoon to scoop out guacamole, shape it into a ball, and then place onto the prepared baking sheet.
5. Prepare remaining guacamole balls in the same manner, cover the balls with aluminum foil, and then freeze for a minimum of 4 hours or overnight.

6. Then switch on the air fryer, insert fryer basket, grease it with olive oil, then shut with its lid, set the fryer at 220 degrees F, and preheat for 5 minutes.
7. In the meantime, crack the egg in a bowl, add egg white and whisk until combined.
8. Place bread crumbs in a shallow dish and then place almond flour in another shallow dish.
9. Working on one guacamole ball at a time, first spray the ball with oil, then coat with almond flour, dip into the egg mixture, then dredge with parmesan cheese and place the ball into heated fryer basket.
10. Fill the fryer basket with more guacamole balls in the single layer, spray with olive oil, close with its lid and cook for 8 minutes until nicely golden and crispy, shaking the basket halfway through.
11. When air fryer beeps, open its lid, transfer guacamole balls onto a serving plate, cook remaining guacamole balls in the same manner and serve.

Nutrition Value:

- Calories: 179 Cal
- Fat: 13 g
- Carbs: 14 g
- Protein: 6 g
- Fiber: 6 g

German Pancakes

Preparation time: 10 minutes
Cooking time: 18 minutes
Servings: 5

Ingredients:

- 1 cup oat flour
- 1/16 teaspoon salt
- 2 tablespoons olive oil
- 3 eggs
- 1 cup coconut milk, unsweetened
- Fresh berries, as needed for garnishing
- Swerve confectioners' sugar, as needed for garnish

Method:

1. Switch on the air fryer, insert fryer basket, then shut with its lid, set the fryer at 390 degrees F, and preheat for 10 minutes.
2. Meanwhile, place all the ingredients in a blender, except for garnishing ones, and pulse until smooth; add 1 tablespoon of coconut milk if the batter is too thick.
3. Take a heatproof ramekin, grease it with olive oil, then pour in pancake batter and spread it evenly.
4. Open the fryer, add ramekin in it, close with its lid and cook for 6 to 8 minutes until the pancake has cooked and the top is golden brown.
5. When air fryer beeps, open its lid, take out the ramekin, then top with berries, and sprinkle with swerve confectioners' and serve.

Nutrition Value:

- Calories: 139 Cal
- Fat: 4 g
- Carbs: 18 g
- Protein: 8 g
- Fiber: 3 g

Tofu Scramble

Preparation time: 10 minutes
Cooking time: 30 minutes
Servings: 3

Ingredients:

- 4 cups broccoli florets
- 1 block tofu, drained, pressed, 1-inch cubed
- 2 1/2 cups chopped red potato, 1-inch cubed
- 1/2 cup chopped red onion
- 1/2 teaspoon garlic powder
- 1/2 teaspoon onion powder
- 1 teaspoon ground turmeric
- 2 tablespoons soy sauce
- 2 tablespoons olive oil

Method:

1. Place tofu pieces in a bowl, add onion, onion powder, garlic powder, and turmeric, drizzle with 1 tablespoon olive oil and soy sauce, toss until well coated, and set aside to marinate until required.
2. Switch on the air fryer, insert fryer basket, grease it with olive oil, then shut with its lid, set the fryer at 400 degrees F, and preheat for 5 minutes.
3. Meanwhile, place potato pieces in a bowl, add remaining oil and toss until well coated.
4. Open the fryer, add potatoes pieces in it, close with its lid and cook for 15 minutes until nicely golden and crispy, shaking the basket every 5 minutes.
5. Then add marinated tofu pieces into the fryer basket, shake well, reserving the marinade, and continue cooking for 10 minutes at 370 degrees F, shaking the basket every 5 minutes.
6. In the meantime, add broccoli florets into the reserved marinade, toss until coated, and set aside until required.
7. After 10 minutes of frying, add broccoli into fryer basket, shake well to mix and cook for 5 minutes
8. When air fryer beeps, open its lid, transfer tofu, potatoes, and broccoli florets onto a serving plate and serve.

Nutrition Value:

- Calories: 276.3 Cal
- Fat: 12.3 g
- Carbs: 29 g
- Protein: 13.1 g
- Fiber: 5 g

Breakfast Biscuits

Preparation time: 10 minutes
Cooking time: 15 minutes
Servings: 9

Ingredients:

- 1 cup almond flour
- 1/4 teaspoon sea salt
- 1/2 teaspoon baking powder
- 2 tablespoons butter, melted
- 2 tablespoons sour cream, non-fat
- 1 cup shredded cheddar cheese, non-fat
- 2 organic eggs

Method:

1. Place flour in a bowl, add salt and baking powder, stir until just mixed and then stir cheese by hand until incorporated.
2. Crack eggs in another bowl, whisk in butter and sour cream until blended, and then slowly stir this mixture with a large fork until sticky batter comes together.
3. Switch on the air fryer, then shut with its lid, set the fryer at 220 degrees F, and preheat for 5 minutes.
4. Meanwhile, take a fryer basket, line it with parchment sheet, and then drop scoops of prepared biscuit batter in a single layer, about ¼ cup of batter for large biscuits or 2 tablespoons of batter for small biscuits.
5. Open the fryer, insert fryer basket in it, close with its lid and cook for 10 minutes for large or 6 minutes for small biscuits until nicely golden and thoroughly cooked.
6. When air fryer beeps, open its lid, transfer biscuits onto a serving plate and serve.

Nutrition Value:

- Calories: 167 Cal
- Fat: 15 g
- Carbs: 3 g
- Protein: 7 g
- Fiber: 1 g

French Toast Sticks

Preparation time: 10 minutes
Cooking time: 17 minutes
Servings: 2

Ingredients:

- 4 slices of almond bread
- 1/16 teaspoon salt
- 1/16 teaspoon ground cloves
- 1/16 teaspoon ground cinnamon
- 1 teaspoon Swerve icing sugar
- 1/16 teaspoon nutmeg
- 2 tablespoons unsalted butter, softened
- 2 eggs, lightly beaten

Method:

1. Crack the eggs in a bowl, whisk until beaten, then add salt, cloves, cinnamon, and nutmeg, and whisk until mixed.
2. Switch on the air fryer, insert fryer basket, grease it with olive oil, then shut with its lid, set the fryer at 350 degrees F, and preheat for 5 minutes.
3. Meanwhile, spread butter on both sides of bread slices, cut the slices into strips and then dredge into the egg batter.
4. Open the fryer, add bread strips in it in a single layer, spray with olive oil, close with its lid and cook for 6 minutes until nicely golden and crispy, flipping and spraying with oil halfway through.
5. When air fryer beeps, open its lid, transfer French toasts onto a serving plate and cook remaining bread strips in the same manner.
6. When done, sprinkle Swerve icing sugar on the French toasts and serve.

Nutrition Value:

- Calories: 178 Cal
- Fat: 15 g
- Carbs: 2 g
- Protein: 5 g
- Fiber: 0.5 g

Frittata

Preparation time: 10 minutes
Cooking time: 14 minutes
Servings: 2

Ingredients:

- 1 ½ stick of Chinese waxed sausage, sliced lengthwise
- ¼ cup chopped kale
- ¼ cup baby spinach leaves
- 2 tablespoons corn
- 1 tablespoon chopped red onion
- 2 tablespoons peas
- 1 small green bell pepper, cored, julienne cut
- 1 medium carrot, peeled, julienne cut
- 1/8 teaspoon salt
- 1/8 teaspoon ground black pepper
- ¼ teaspoon olive oil
- 3 eggs

Method:

1. Switch on the air fryer, then shut with its lid, set the fryer at 350 degrees F, and preheat for 5 minutes.
2. Meanwhile, grease the air fryer baking pan, place sausage in it, add onion, stir until just mixed and spread evenly.
3. Open the fryer, insert baking pan in it, close with its lid and cook for 4 minutes.
4. Meanwhile, place the remaining ingredients in a bowl and whisk well until combined.
5. When air fryer beeps, open its lid, pour in the prepared batter, and continue cooking for 4 minutes.
6. Then increase air frying temperature to 390 degrees F and cook for 1 minute until the top of the frittata is nicely browned.
7. When air fryer beeps, open its lid, take out the baking pan, transfer frittata onto a serving plate, then cut it into slices and serve.

Nutrition Value:

- Calories: 290.5 Cal
- Fat: 19.7 g
- Carbs: 11 g
- Protein: 17.4 g
- Fiber: 2 g

Breakfast Bombs

Preparation time: 10 minutes
Cooking time: 40 minutes
Servings: 4

Ingredients:

- 4 ounces whole-wheat pizza dough
- 3 slices of bacon, center-cut
- 1 tablespoon chopped fresh chives
- 3 large eggs, beaten
- 1-ounce cream cheese, softened, low-fat

Method:

1. Take a skillet pan, place it over medium heat, add bacon, and cook for 10 minutes until very crispy.
2. Then transfer bacon to a cutting board, let it cool for 3 minutes and then crumble it, set aside until required.
3. Pour beaten eggs into the skillet pan, stir and cook for 1 minute until eggs are almost set.
4. Transfer eggs into a bowl, add bacon, chives, and cream cheese and stir well until combined.
5. Switch on the air fryer, insert fryer basket, grease it with olive oil, then shut with its lid, set the fryer at 350 degrees F, and preheat for 5 minutes.
6. Meanwhile, divide pizza dough into four sections, roll each section into the 5-inch round crust, and then add one-fourth of the cooked egg mixture into the center of each crust.
7. Brush the edges of the crust with water and then form a purse by wrapping crust around the egg mixture.
8. Open the fryer, add crust in it in a single layer, then spray with olive oil, close with its lid and cook for 6 minutes until nicely golden brown.
9. When air fryer beeps, open its lid, transfer the breakfast bomb onto a serving plate and cook the remaining crust in the same manner.
10. Serve straight away.

Nutrition Value:

- Calories: 305 Cal
- Fat: 15 g
- Carbs: 26 g
- Protein: 19 g
- Fiber: 2 g

Bacon with Eggs

Preparation time: 5 minutes
Cooking time: 23 minutes
Servings: 1

Ingredients:

- 2 slices of bacon, thick-cut
- 2 eggs
- ¼ teaspoon salt
- ¼ teaspoon ground black pepper
- 2 tablespoons unsalted butter

Method:

1. Switch on the air fryer, insert fryer basket, grease it with olive oil, then shut with its lid, set the fryer at 400 degrees F, and preheat for 5 minutes.
2. Then open the fryer, add bacon slices in it in a single layer, close with its lid and cook for 10 minutes until crispy and done, shaking the basket every 5 minutes.
3. When air fryer beeps, open its lid, transfer bacon onto a serving plate and set aside until required.
4. Replace fryer basket with air fryer baking pan, add butter in it, then shut with its lid, set the fryer at 400 degrees F, and cook for 1 minute until the butter has melted.
5. Crack eggs in the baking pan, switch temperature to 325 degrees F, close air fryer with lid and cook for 6 to 8 minutes or until eggs are fried to the desired level.
6. When air fryer beeps, open its lid, transfer fried eggs onto a serving plate and serve with bacon.

Nutrition Value:

- Calories: 487 Cal
- Fat: 44.4 g
- Carbs: 1.2 g
- Protein: 20.7 g
- Fiber: 0 g

Omelet

Preparation time: 5 minutes
Cooking time: 15 minutes
Servings: 1

Ingredients:

- 2 tablespoons chopped ham
- 2 tablespoons chopped red bell pepper
- 2 tablespoons sliced green onion
- 1 tablespoon chopped mushroom
- ¼ teaspoon salt
- 1 teaspoon breakfast seasoning
- 2 eggs
- ¼ cup coconut milk, unsweetened
- 2 tablespoons grated cheddar cheese
- 2 tablespoons grated mozzarella cheese

Method:

1. Switch on the air fryer, insert fryer baking pan, grease it with olive oil, then shut with its lid, set the fryer at 350 degrees F, and preheat for 5 minutes.
2. Meanwhile, place crack eggs in a bowl, whisk them until beaten, then add ham, pepper, onion, mushrooms, and salt and whisk until just mixed.
3. Open the fryer, pour in egg mixture, close with its lid and cook for 5 minutes.
4. Then sprinkle breakfast seasoning on top, scatter with cheeses and continue cooking for 5 minutes until cheese has melted and omelet has cooked.
5. When air fryer beeps, open its lid, take out the baking pan, slide omelet onto a serving plate and serve.

Nutrition Value:

- Calories: 350 Cal
- Fat: 16 g
- Carbs: 19 g
- Protein: 6 g
- Fiber: 2 g

Hash Browns

Preparation time: 30 minutes
Cooking time: 35 minutes |
Servings: 2

Ingredients:

- 1 small red onion, peeled, 1-inch sliced
- 1 1/2 pounds potatoes, peeled
- 1 medium red bell pepper, deseeded, 1-inch cubed
- 1 jalapeno, deseeded, cut into 1-inch rings
- 1/8 teaspoon salt
- 1/2 teaspoon ground cumin
- 1/8 teaspoon ground black pepper
- 1/2 teaspoon taco seasoning mix
- 1 1/2 tablespoon olive oil

Method:

1. Cut potatoes into 1-inch cubes, place them in a bowl, cover them with chilled water and let soak for 20 minutes.
2. Then switch on the air fryer, insert fryer basket, grease it with olive oil, then shut with its lid, set the fryer at 320 degrees F, and preheat for 5 minutes.
3. Meanwhile, drain the potatoes, pat dry with paper towels, place them in a bowl, drizzle with 1 tablespoon oil and toss until coated.
4. Open the fryer, add potatoes in it, close with its lid and cook for 18 minutes until nicely golden, shaking the basket every 5 minutes.
5. In the meantime, add onion, bell pepper, and jalapeno into the bowl that was used for potatoes, drizzle remaining oil over vegetables, season with salt, taco seasoning, black pepper, and cumin and toss until well coated.
6. When potatoes are done, add them to the bowl containing vegetable mixture and toss until mixed.
7. Return fryer basket into the air fryer, grease it with olive oil, then shut with its lid, set the fryer at 356 degrees F, and preheat for 5 minutes.
8. Then open the fryer, add the vegetable mixture in it, close with its lid and cook for 12 minutes until nicely golden and crispy, shaking the basket every 5 minutes.

9. When air fryer beeps, open its lid, transfer hash browns onto a serving plate and serve.

Nutrition Value:

- Calories: 186 Cal
- Fat: 4.3 g
- Carbs: 4 g
- Protein: 4 g
- Fiber: 4.8 g

Chapter 7: Poultry

Mediterranean Breaded Chicken

Preparation time: 10 minutes
Cooking time: 30 minutes
Servings: 2

Ingredients:

- 2 large chicken breast, cut into nugget-style pieces
- ½ teaspoon salt
- 1 tablespoon dried thyme
- ½ teaspoon ground black pepper
- 3 ounces Tuscan herb granola
- 1 egg

Method:

1. Switch on the air fryer, insert fryer basket, grease it with olive oil, then shut with its lid, set the fryer at 350 degrees F, and preheat for 10 minutes.
2. Meanwhile, crack the egg in a bowl, whisk it until beaten and set aside until required.
3. Take granola in a plastic bag, seal it and then bash it with a rolling pin until the mixture resembles medium pieces.
4. Add salt, thyme, and black pepper into the granola, seal the bag and shake it until mixed.
5. Coat chicken pieces in the egg, then add them into the granola mixture, seal the bag and shake it until chicken pieces are evenly coated.
6. Open the fryer, add chicken nuggets in it in a single layer, spray with oil, close with its lid and cook for 20 minutes until nicely golden and crispy, shaking the basket every 5 minutes.
7. When air fryer beeps, open its lid, transfer chicken nuggets onto a serving plate and serve.

Nutrition Value:

- Calories: 453.5 Cal
- Fat: 17.1 g
- Carbs: 22.7 g
- Protein: 52.2 g
- Fiber: 2.7 g

Chicken Drumstick

Preparation time: 10 minutes
Cooking time: 25 minutes
Servings: 4

Ingredients:

- 2 1/2 pounds chicken drumsticks
- 1/4 cup coconut flour
- 1/2 teaspoon garlic powder
- 1/2 teaspoon sea salt
- 1 teaspoon smoked paprika
- 1/4 teaspoon ground black pepper
- 1/4 teaspoon dried thyme
- 2 large eggs
- 1 cup pork rinds

Method:

1. Place coconut flour in a shallow dish, add salt and black pepper and stir until mixed.
2. Crack eggs in another dish and then whisk until beaten.
3. Place pork rinds in another dish, add garlic, thyme, and pork rinds and stir until mixed.
4. Switch on the air fryer, insert fryer basket, grease it with olive oil, then shut with its lid, set the fryer at 400 degrees F, and preheat for 5 minutes.
5. Meanwhile, first coat chicken drumsticks into the coconut flour mixture, then dip into the eggs and dredge into pork rind mixture until evenly coated.
6. Open the fryer, add chicken drumsticks in it in a single layer, spray with olive oil, close with its lid and cook for 20 minutes until crispy and cooked, shaking the basket every 5 minutes.
7. When air fryer beeps, open its lid, transfer chicken drumsticks onto a serving plate, and cooking remaining drumsticks in the same manner.
8. Serve straight away.

Nutrition Value:

- Calories: 273 Cal

- Fat: 15 g
- Carbs: 3 g
- Protein: 28 g
- Fiber: 1 g

Chicken Breast

Preparation time: 5 minutes
Cooking time: 15 minutes
Servings: 1

Ingredients:

- 7 ounces chicken breast, skinless
- 1 teaspoon chicken seasoning
- 2 teaspoons olive oil
- Mediterranean salad for serving

Method:

1. Switch on the air fryer, insert fryer basket, grease it with olive oil, then shut with its lid, set the fryer at 390 degrees F, and preheat for 5 minutes.
2. Meanwhile, coat chicken with oil and then season them with chicken seasoning on both sides.
3. Open the fryer, add chicken breasts in it, close with its lid and cook for 15 minutes until nicely golden and thoroughly cooked, shaking the basket every 5 minutes and flipping the chicken breast halfway through.
4. When air fryer beeps, open its lid, transfer chicken breast onto a cutting board, let it cool for 5 minutes and then cut it into slices.
5. Serve chicken with Mediterranean salad.

Nutrition Value:

- Calories: 262 Cal
- Fat: 6 g
- Carbs: 1 g
- Protein: 48 g
- Fiber: 0 g

Thai Chili Fried Chicken Wings

Preparation time: 40 minutes
Cooking time: 30 minutes
Servings: 2

Ingredients:

- 16 chicken wings
- 1/2 cup almond flour
- 2 ½ teaspoons chicken seasoning
- 1/4 cup buttermilk, low-fat

For Thai Chili Marinade:

- 2 green onions, chopped
- 1 teaspoon grated ginger
- 1 ½ teaspoon minced garlic
- 1 teaspoon honey
- 3 tablespoons soy sauce
- 1 teaspoon of rice wine vinegar
- 1 tablespoon Sriracha sauce
- 1 tablespoon sesame oil

Method:

1. Prepare the marinade, and for this, place all its ingredients in a blender and pulse for 1 minute until blended.
2. Pat dry chicken wings, place them in a large plastic bag, pour in the buttermilk, then add chicken seasoning, seal the bag, turn it upside down until chicken wings have coated, and then marinate in the refrigerator for a minimum of 30 minutes.
3. Once the chicken wings have marinated, switch on the air fryer, insert fryer basket, grease it with olive oil, then shut with its lid, set the fryer at 400 degrees F, and preheat for 5 minutes.
4. Meanwhile, place flour in another plastic bag, add marinated chicken wings in it, then seal the bag and shake until chicken wings have evenly coated with almond flour.

5. Open the fryer, stack chicken wings in it, spray with olive oil, close with its lid and cook for 15 minutes until nicely golden and thoroughly cooked, shaking the basket every 5 minutes and flipping the chicken wings halfway through.
6. When air fryer beeps, open its lid, take out the chicken wings and brush well with the prepared marinade.
7. Return chicken wings into the air fryer, shut with lid, and continue cooking for 7 to 10 minutes until glazed.
8. Serve straight away.

Nutrition Value:

- Calories: 202 Cal
- Fat: 11 g
- Carbs: 12 g
- Protein: 12 g
- Fiber: 2 g

Buffalo Chicken Wings

Preparation time: 5 minutes
Cooking time: 55 minutes
Servings: 4

Ingredients:

- 2 ½ pounds chicken wings
- 1 tablespoon olive oil

For Buffalo Sauce:

- 1 teaspoon garlic powder
- 1/4 teaspoon cayenne pepper
- 2 tablespoons apple cider vinegar
- 2/3 cup cayenne pepper sauce
- 1/2 cup unsalted butter, softened

Method:

1. Switch on the air fryer, insert fryer basket, grease it with olive oil, then shut with its lid, set the fryer at 360 degrees F, and preheat for 5 minutes.
2. Meanwhile, place chicken wings in a large bowl, add olive oil and massage it until evenly coated.
3. Open the fryer, add chicken wings in it in a single layer, close with its lid and cook for 25 minutes until nicely golden and thoroughly cooked, shaking the basket every 5 minutes and flipping the chicken wings halfway through.
4. Meanwhile, prepare buffalo sauce and for this, place a saucepan over medium heat, add all its ingredients in it, whisk well and cook for 3 to 5 minutes until sauce is warm through, set aside until required and keep it warm.
5. When air fryer beeps, open its lid, transfer fried chicken wings onto a plate, and cook remaining chicken wings in the same manner.
6. Add chicken wings into the sauce, toss until well coated and serve.

Nutrition Value:

- Calories: 481 Cal
- Fat: 41.5 g
- Carbs: 7.3 g
- Protein: 20.7 g
- Fiber: 0.1 g

Chicken Fajita Rollups

Preparation time: 15 minutes
Cooking time: 17 minutes
Servings: 6

Ingredients:

- 1/2 of large yellow bell pepper, cored, cut into strips
- 3 large chicken breasts
- 1/2 of large red bell pepper, cored, cut into strips
- 1/2 large red onion, peeled, sliced
- 1/2 of large green bell pepper, cored, cut into strips

For Spice Mix:

- 1 teaspoon garlic powder
- 2 teaspoons paprika
- ¾ teaspoon salt
- 1 teaspoon cumin powder
- 1/2 teaspoon cayenne pepper
- ¼ teaspoon ground black pepper
- 1/2 teaspoon dried oregano

Method:

1. Prepare spice mix and for this, place all its ingredients in a bowl and stir until mixed, set aside until required.
2. Slice each chicken breast in half lengthwise, then cover each chicken slice in a plastic wrap or place it between two parchment papers and pound with a meat mallet until ¼-inch thick.
3. Prepare rolls and for this, season both sides of chicken breast with prepare spice mix, then divide six strips of bell peppers of each color and onion slices on one side of chicken, then roll tightly and secure with a toothpick.
4. Then switch on the air fryer, insert fryer basket, grease it with olive oil, then shut with its lid, set the fryer at 400 degrees F, and preheat for 5 minutes.
5. Open the fryer, add chicken rolls in it, spray them with olive oil, close with its lid and cook for 12 minutes until nicely golden and cooked thoroughly, shaking the basket every 5 minutes and turning rolls halfway.

6. When air fryer beeps, open its lid, transfer chicken fajita rolls onto a serving plate and serve.

Nutrition Value:

- Calories: 138.2 Cal
- Fat: 3.4 g
- Carbs: 4.1 g
- Protein: 22.8 g
- Fiber: 1.2 g

Tso's Chicken

Preparation time: 15 minutes
Cooking time: 45 minutes
Servings: 4

Ingredients:

- 1 pound chicken thighs, boneless, skinless, cut into1 to 1 1/4-inch chunk
- 2 tablespoons sliced green onion, divided
- 3 chiles de árbol, deseeded, chopped
- 1 tablespoon grated ginger
- 1 tablespoon minced garlic
- 1/4 teaspoon salt
- 1/4 teaspoon ground white pepper
- 1/3 cup and 2 teaspoons cornstarch, divided
- 2 teaspoons erythritol sweetener
- 2 teaspoons rice vinegar
- 1 1/2 tablespoons olive oil
- 1 teaspoon toasted sesame oil
- 2 tablespoons soy sauce
- 2 tablespoons ketchup
- 1 egg
- 7 tablespoons chicken broth
- 1/2 teaspoon toasted sesame seeds

Method:

1. Switch on the air fryer, insert fryer basket, grease it with olive oil, then shut with its lid, set the fryer at 400 degrees F, and preheat for 5 minutes.
2. Meanwhile, crack the egg in a large bowl and whisk until slightly beaten.
3. Cut chicken into 1 ¼-inch piece, add to the egg and toss until coated.
4. Place 1/3 cup cornstarch in a shallow dish, add salt and black pepper, stir well, then add chicken and stir until each chicken piece has coated.
5. Open the fryer, add chicken pieces in it in a single layer, spray them with oil, close with its lid and cook for 15 minutes until nicely golden and cooked, shaking the basket every 5 minutes and turning chicken pieces halfway through.

6. When air fryer beeps, open its lid, transfer chicken pieces onto a plate, and cook remaining chicken pieces in the same manner.
7. Meanwhile, place remaining cornstarch in a bowl, add sweetener, vinegar, soy sauce, ketchup, and chicken broth, whisk well, and set aside until required.
8. When all chicken pieces have cooked, place a large skillet pan over medium heat, add oil and when hot, add chilies and cook for 2 minutes until it starts to sizzles.
9. Add ginger and garlic, cook for 1 minute until fragrant, then pour in cornstarch mixture and stir well.
10. Switch heat to medium-high level, cook for 3 minutes until the sauce starts to bubble, then add chicken, stir until coated, and cook for 2 minutes until the sauce has thickened.
11. Remove skillet pan from the heat, add 1 tablespoon green onion, drizzle with sesame sauce, stir until mixed, and transfer chicken to a serving dish.
12. Sprinkle with sesame seeds, garnish with remaining green onion and serve.

Nutrition Value:

- Calories: 302 Cal
- Fat: 13 g
- Carbs: 18 g
- Protein: 26 g
- Fiber: 0 g

Lemon Pepper Chicken

Preparation time: 10 minutes
Cooking time: 19 minutes
Servings: 6

Ingredients:

- 6 large skinless chicken breasts
- 3 tablespoons lemon pepper seasoning
- 2 teaspoons Worcestershire sauce
- 1 teaspoon salt
- ¼ cup lemon juice
- ¼ cup olive oil

Method:

1. Cut chicken into bite-size pieces, add them into a large bowl, then add remaining ingredients, stir until well coated, and let marinate for a minimum in the refrigerator.
2. When the chicken has marinated, switch on the air fryer, insert fryer basket, grease it with olive oil, then shut with its lid, set the fryer at 350 degrees F, and preheat for 5 minutes.
3. Open the fryer, add chicken pieces in it, close with its lid and cook for 14 minutes until nicely golden and cooked through, shaking the basket every 5 minutes, flipping chicken and spraying with oil halfway.
4. When air fryer beeps, open its lid, transfer chicken onto a serving plate and serve.

Nutrition Value:

- Calories: 149.4 Cal
- Fat: 1.7 g
- Carbs: 3.2 g
- Protein: 29.6 g
- Fiber: 0.9 g

Caribbean Spiced Chicken

Preparation time: 10 minutes
Cooking time: 25 minutes
Servings: 8

Ingredients:

- 3 pounds chicken thigh, boneless, skinless
- 1 1/2 teaspoons ground ginger
- 1 tablespoon ground cinnamon
- 1 ½ teaspoon salt
- 1 tablespoon cayenne pepper
- 1 tablespoon ground coriander
- 1 teaspoon ground black pepper
- 1 1/2 teaspoons ground nutmeg
- 4 tablespoon olive oil

Method:

1. Pat dry chicken, then season with salt and black pepper on both sides and let it marinate for 30 minutes at room temperature.
2. Then switch on the air fryer, insert fryer basket, grease it with olive oil, then shut with its lid, set the fryer at 390 degrees F, and preheat for 5 minutes.
3. Meanwhile, brush chicken with oil and then season with remaining spices.
4. Open the fryer, add chicken thighs in it in a single layer, close with its lid and cook for 10 minutes until nicely golden and thoroughly cooked, shaking the basket every 5 minutes and turning the chicken halfway through.
5. When air fryer beeps, open its lid, transfer chicken onto a plate, wrap with aluminum foil to keep it warm, and cook the remaining chicken in the same manner.
6. Serve straight away.

Nutrition Value:

- Calories: 202 Cal
- Fat: 13.4 g
- Carbs: 1.7 g
- Protein: 25 g
- Fiber: 0.4 g

Fennel Chicken

Preparation time: 40 minutes
Cooking time: 35 minutes
Servings: 4

Ingredients:

- 1 pound chicken thighs, boneless, skinless
- 1 large red onion, peeled, 1-1/2 inch sliced
- 2 teaspoons lemon juice
- 1/4 cup chopped cilantro

For Marinade:

- 2 teaspoons minced ginger
- 2 teaspoons minced garlic
- 1 teaspoon salt
- 1 teaspoon cayenne pepper
- 1 teaspoon turmeric
- 1 teaspoon smoked paprika
- 1 teaspoon garam masala
- 1 teaspoon ground fennel seeds
- 1 tablespoon olive oil

Method:

1. Prepare the marinade and for this, place all its ingredients in a large bowl and stir until combined.
2. Pierce chicken thighs with a fork, then add to marinade along with onion, toss until well coated and marinate for a minimum of 30 minutes in the refrigerator.
3. When chicken and vegetables have marinated, switch on the air fryer, insert fryer basket, grease it with olive oil, then shut with its lid, set the fryer at 360 degrees F, and preheat for 5 minutes.
4. Open the fryer, add chicken and onions in it, spray with olive oil, close with its lid and cook for 15 minutes until nicely golden and cooked, shaking the basket every 5 minutes.
5. When air fryer beeps, open its lid, transfer chicken and vegetables onto a serving plate, drizzle with lemon juice, sprinkle with cilantro, and serve.

Nutrition Value:

- Calories: 190 Cal
- Fat: 100 g
- Carbs: 100 g
- Protein: 100 g
- Fiber: 100 g

Chapter 8: Appetizers and Siders

Patatas Bravas

Preparation time: 25 minutes
Cooking time: 20 minutes
Servings: 4

Ingredients:

- 12 ounces red potato, cut into 1-inch chunks
- 1/2 teaspoon ground black pepper
- 1/2 teaspoon sea salt
- 1 teaspoon garlic powder
- 1/2 teaspoon cayenne pepper
- 1 tablespoon smoked paprika
- 1 tablespoon coconut oil
- ¼ teaspoon dried chives
- Garlic aioli for serving

Method:

1. Take a pot, place it half-full with water over medium heat, bring the water to boil, add potato pieces, and cook for 6 minutes.
2. Then drain the potatoes, pat them dry, cool for 15 minutes and add them into a large bowl.
3. Add garlic into the potatoes, season with 1/8 teaspoon each of salt and black pepper, drizzle with oil and toss until coated.
4. Switch on the air fryer, insert fryer basket, grease it with olive oil, then shut with its lid, set the fryer at 390 degrees F, and preheat for 5 minutes.
5. Open the fryer, add potatoes in it in a single layer, spray them with olive oil, close with its lid and cook for 15 minutes until nicely golden and crispy, shaking the basket halfway through.
6. When air fryer beeps, open its lid, transfer potatoes to a bowl, add remaining ingredients, toss until coated, and serve them with garlic aioli.

Nutrition Value:

- Calories: 97 Cal

- Fat: 4 g
- Carbs: 15 g
- Protein: 1 g
- Fiber: 1 g

Cauliflower

Preparation time: 5 minutes
Cooking time: 20 minutes
Servings: 5

Ingredients:

- 16 ounces cauliflower, cut into florets
- 2/3 teaspoon salt
- ½ teaspoon ground black pepper
- 2 teaspoons olive oil
- 1 tablespoon potato starch

Method:

1. Switch on the air fryer, insert fryer basket, grease it with olive oil, then shut with its lid, set the fryer at 400 degrees F, and preheat for 5 minutes.
2. Meanwhile, place cauliflower florets in a bowl, add remaining ingredients and toss until well coated.
3. Open the fryer, add cauliflower florets in it, close with its lid and cook for 15 minutes until nicely golden and crispy, shaking the basket every 5 minutes.
4. When air fryer beeps, open its lid, transfer cauliflower florets onto a serving plate and serve.

Nutrition Value:

- Calories: 36 Cal
- Fat: 1 g
- Carbs: 5 g
- Protein: 1 g
- Fiber: 1 g

Onion Rings

Preparation time: 10 minutes
Cooking time: 22 minutes
Servings: 4

Ingredients:

- 1 large white onion, peeled, sliced into ½-inch thick rings
- 2/3 cup pork rinds
- 3 tablespoons coconut flour
- 3 tablespoons almond flour
- 1/2 teaspoon garlic powder
- 1/4 teaspoon sea salt
- 1/2 teaspoon paprika
- 2 eggs

Method:

1. Take a shallow dish, place coconut flour in it, add salt, stir until mixed and set aside until required.
2. Crack eggs in a bowl, whisk until combined, and set aside until required.
3. Place pork rinds in another shallow dish, add almond flour in it, season with garlic powder and paprika, and stir until mixed.
4. Switch on the air fryer, insert fryer basket, grease it with olive oil, then shut with its lid, set the fryer at 400 degrees F, and preheat for 5 minutes.
5. Meanwhile, prepare onion rings and for this, dredge them in coconut flour, dip them into beaten eggs and then coat with pork rind mixture.
6. Open the fryer, add onion rings in it in a single layer, spray olive oil, close with its lid and cook for 16 minutes until nicely golden and crispy, shaking the basket every 5 minutes.
7. When air fryer beeps, open its lid, transfer onion rings onto a serving plate, keep them warm and cook remaining onion rings in the same manner.
8. Serve straight away.

Nutrition Value:

- Calories: 135 Cal
- Fat: 7 g
- Carbs: 8 g
- Protein: 8 g
- Fiber: 3 g

Spicy Chicken Thighs

Preparation time: 10 minutes
Cooking time: 45 minutes
Servings: 4

Ingredients:

- 2 pounds chicken thighs, bone-in, skin-on
- 2 tablespoons sliced green onions, for garnish
- 1 teaspoon toasted sesame seeds, for garnish

For the Marinade:

- 1 teaspoon minced garlic
- 2 teaspoons grated ginger
- 2 tablespoons honey
- 1/3 cup soy sauce
- 1/4 cup olive oil
- 2 tablespoons chili garlic sauce
- 1 lime, juiced

Method:

1. Prepare the marinade and for this, place all its ingredients in a bowl and stir until combined.
2. Reserve half of the marinade, then pour remaining marinade in a bowl, add chicken thighs in it, toss until well coated and marinate in the refrigerator for 30 minutes.
3. Then switch on the air fryer, insert fryer basket, grease it with olive oil, then shut with its lid, set the fryer at 400 degrees F, and preheat for 5 minutes.
4. Open the fryer, add chicken thighs in it in a single layer, close with its lid and cook for 20 minutes until nicely golden and crispy, turning chicken thighs halfway through.
5. Meanwhile, pour remaining marinade in a saucepan, place it over medium heat, bring it to boil, and cook for 5 minutes until slightly thick, set aside until required.
6. When air fryer beeps, open its lid, transfer chicken thighs onto a serving plate, keep them warm and cook remaining chicken thighs in the same manner.

7. When done, brush chicken thighs generously with prepared sauce, sprinkle with green onion and sesame seeds, and serve.

Nutrition Value:

- Calories: 287 Cal
- Fat: 18.8 g
- Carbs: 3.6 g
- Protein: 26.5 g
- Fiber: 0.5 g

Zucchini, Yellow Squash, and Carrots

Preparation time: 10 minutes
Cooking time: 40 minutes
Servings: 4

Ingredients:

- 1 pound zucchini, ends trimmed, cut into ¾-inch half moons
- ½ pound carrots, peeled, 1-inch cubed
- 1 pound yellow squash, ends trimmed, cut into ¾-inch half moons
- 1 tablespoon chopped tarragon
- ½ teaspoon ground white pepper
- 1 teaspoon salt
- 6 teaspoons olive oil

Method:

1. Switch on the air fryer, insert fryer basket, grease it with olive oil, then shut with its lid, set the fryer at 400 degrees F, and preheat for 5 minutes.
2. Meanwhile, place carrots in a bowl, drizzle with 2 teaspoon oil, and toss until combined.
3. Open the fryer, add carrot pieces in it, close with its lid and cook for 5 minutes until nicely golden and crispy, shaking the basket halfway through.
4. Meanwhile, place zucchini and squash pieces in a bowl, add remaining ingredients except for tarragon and toss until mixed.
5. When air fryer beeps, open the lid, add zucchini and squash into fryer basket, shut with its lid and cook for 30 minutes until nicely golden and crispy, shaking the basket every 10 minutes.
6. When done, transfer vegetables into a bowl, top with tarragon leaves and serve.

Nutrition Value:

- Calories: 121.5 Cal
- Fat: 7.4 g
- Carbs: 11.5 g
- Protein: 2.1 g
- Fiber: 4 g

Mac and Cheese

Preparation time: 10 minutes
Cooking time: 30 minutes
Servings: 2

Ingredients:

- 1 cup elbow macaroni, whole-wheat
- 1/2 cup broccoli florets
- ¼ teaspoon ground black pepper
- 1/3 teaspoon salt
- 1 1/2 cup grated cheddar cheese
- 1 tablespoon grated parmesan cheese
- 1/2 cup almond milk, warmed

Method:

1. Take a pot half full with water, place it over medium-high heat, bring it to boil, then add macaroni and broccoli and cook for 10 minutes until tender.
2. When done, drain macaroni and vegetables, transfer them in a bowl, pour in milk, add cheddar cheese, season with black pepper and salt, and stir until well mixed.
3. Switch on the air fryer, insert fryer basket, then shut with its lid, set the fryer at 350 degrees F, and preheat for 5 minutes.
4. Meanwhile, place mac and cheese mixture in a heatproof baking dish that fits into the air fryer and sprinkle parmesan cheese on top.
5. Open the fryer, place baking dish in it, close with its lid and cook for 15 minutes until pasta is bubbling.
6. When air fryer beeps, open its lid, take out the baking dish, let the pasta sit for 10 minutes, and then serve.

Nutrition Value:

- Calories: 320 Cal
- Fat: 17 g
- Carbs: 29 g
- Protein: 15 g
- Fiber: 2.8 g

Whole-Wheat Pizzas

Preparation time: 10 minutes
Cooking time: 25 minutes
Servings: 2

Ingredients:

- 2 whole-wheat pita rounds
- 1 small tomato, cut into eight slices
- ½ teaspoon minced garlic
- 1 cup baby spinach leaves
- 1/4 cup marinara sauce
- 1/4 cup shredded mozzarella cheese
- 1 tablespoon grated parmesan cheese

Method:

1. Switch on the air fryer, insert fryer basket, grease it with olive oil, then shut with its lid, set the fryer at 350 degrees F, and preheat for 10 minutes.
2. Meanwhile, prepare pizzas and for this, spread 1 tablespoon of marinara sauce on one side of each pita bread, then evenly top with spinach and tomatoes, and then sprinkle with garlic and cheeses.
3. Open the fryer, add one pizza in it, close with its lid and cook for 5 minutes until nicely golden and crispy.
4. When air fryer beeps, open its lid, transfer the pizza onto a serving plate, keep it warm, and cook remaining pizza in the same manner.
5. Serve straight away.

Nutrition Value:

- Calories: 229 Cal
- Fat: 5 g
- Carbs: 37 g
- Protein: 11 g
- Fiber: 5 g

Chicken Nuggets

Preparation time: 10 minutes
Cooking time: 35 minutes
Servings: 6

Ingredients:

- 1 cup almond flour
- 2 pounds of chicken breast
- 1/2 teaspoon garlic powder
- 1 teaspoon onion flakes
- 1/2 teaspoon salt
- 4 tablespoons olive oil
- 1 egg, beaten

Method:

1. Take a shallow dish, add flour in it, season with onion powder, salt, and garlic and stir well.
2. Crack the egg in a bowl, add oil, and whisk well until incorporated.
3. Cut chicken breast into bite-size pieces, then dredge with almond flour mixture and coat with egg mixture.
4. Switch on the air fryer, insert fryer basket, grease it with olive oil, then shut with its lid, set the fryer at 350 degrees F, and preheat for 5 minutes.
5. Open the fryer, add chicken nuggets in it in a single layer, close with its lid and cook for 15 minutes until nicely golden and crispy, shaking the basket every 5 minutes and turning chicken nuggets halfway through.
6. When air fryer beeps, open its lid, transfer chicken nuggets onto a serving plate, keep them warm and cook remaining chicken nuggets in the same manner.
7. Serve straight away.

Nutrition Value:

- Calories: 445 Cal
- Fat: 25.5 g
- Carbs: 4.5 g
- Protein: 48.8 g
- Fiber: 2 g

Sweet Potato Cauliflower Patties

Preparation time: 15 minutes
Cooking time: 52 minutes
Servings: 10

Ingredients:

- 1 large sweet potato, peeled, diced
- 2 cup cauliflower florets
- 1 green onion, chopped
- 1 cup cilantro
- 1 teaspoon minced garlic
- 1/4 teaspoon salt
- 1/4 teaspoon ground black pepper
- 2 tablespoons ranch seasoning mix
- 2 tablespoons arrowroot starch
- 1/2 teaspoon red chili powder
- 1/4 cup ground flaxseed
- 1/4 teaspoon cumin
- 1/4 cup sunflower seeds

Method:

1. Place sweet potato pieces in a food processor and pulse until coarsely chopped.
2. Then add cauliflower florets along with garlic and onion and pulse again until combined.
3. Add remaining, pulse for 1 minute until thick batter comes together, then shape the batter into 8 to 10 patties and freeze them for 10 minutes.
4. Switch on the air fryer, insert fryer basket, grease it with olive oil, then shut with its lid, set the fryer at 370 degrees F, and preheat for 5 minutes.
5. Open the fryer, add prepared patties in it in a single layer, spray them with oil, close with its lid, and cook for 18 minutes until nicely golden and crispy, turning the patties halfway through.
6. When air fryer beeps, open its lid, transfer patties onto a serving plate, keep them warm and cook remaining patties in the same manner.
7. Serve straight away.

Nutrition Value:

- Calories: 85 Cal
- Fat: 3 g
- Carbs: 9 g
- Protein: 2.7 g
- Fiber: 3.5 g

Cauliflower Rice

Preparation time: 10 minutes
Cooking time: 27 minutes
Servings: 3

Ingredients:

- 6 ounces tofu, pressed, drained
- 1/2 cup diced white onion
- 1/2 cup frozen peas
- 3 cups riced cauliflower
- 1/2 cup chopped broccoli florets
- 1 cup diced carrot
- 1 tablespoon minced ginger
- 1 teaspoon minced garlic
- 1 teaspoon turmeric powder
- 1 tablespoon apple cider vinegar
- 4 tablespoons soy sauce
- 1 1/2 teaspoons toasted sesame oil

Method:

1. Switch on the air fryer, insert fryer baking pan, grease it with olive oil, then shut with its lid, set the fryer at 370 degrees F, and preheat for 5 minutes.
2. Meanwhile, place them in a large bowl, crumble it, add onion, carrot, sprinkle with turmeric, drizzle with 2 tablespoons soy sauce and toss until mixed.
3. Open the fryer, add tofu in it, spray with olive oil, close with its lid and cook for 10 minutes until nicely golden, shaking the basket halfway through.
4. Meanwhile, place remaining ingredients in a bowl, toss until well mixed and set aside until required.
5. When air fryer beeps, open its lid, add remaining ingredients into the tofu, shake gently until just mixed, close with its lid, and cook for 12 minutes until nicely golden and cooked through, shaking the basket halfway through.
6. Serve straight away.

Nutrition Value:

- Calories: 153 Cal

- Fat: 4 g
- Carbs: 18 g
- Protein: 9 g
- Fiber: 6 g

Chapter 9: Beef, Pork, and Lamb

Meatloaf Sliders

Preparation time: 10 minutes
Cooking time: 30 minutes
Servings: 8

Ingredients:

- 1 pound ground beef
- ½ cup almond flour
- ¼ cup chopped red onion
- ¼ cup coconut flour
- 1 teaspoon minced garlic
- 1 teaspoon Italian seasoning
- ½ teaspoon ground black pepper
- ½ teaspoon of sea salt
- 1 tablespoon Worcestershire sauce
- ½ teaspoon dried tarragon
- 2 eggs, beaten
- ¼ cup ketchup

Method:

1. Place all the ingredients in a large bowl and mix well until combined.
2. Then shape the mixture into eight patties and refrigerate them for 10 minutes until firm.
3. Then switch on the air fryer, insert fryer basket, grease it with olive oil, then shut with its lid, set the fryer at 360 degrees F, and preheat for 10 minutes.
4. Open the fryer, add meatloaf slider in it in a single layer, spray with oil, close with its lid and cook for 10 minutes until nicely golden and thoroughly cooked, shaking the basket every 5 minutes and turning the sliders halfway through.
5. When air fryer beeps, open its lid, transfer sliders onto a serving plate, keep them warm and cook remaining sliders in the same manner.
6. Serve straight away.

Nutrition Value:

- Calories: 228 Cal
- Fat: 17 g
- Carbs: 6 g
- Protein: 13 g
- Fiber: 2 g

Scotch Eggs

Preparation time: 10 minutes
Cooking time: 25 minutes
Servings: 4

Ingredients:

- 1 pound pork sausage
- 1 tablespoon chopped chives
- 1/8 teaspoon salt
- 2 teaspoons ground mustard
- 1/8 teaspoon ground black pepper
- 1/8 teaspoon grated nutmeg
- 2 tablespoons chopped parsley
- 4 eggs, hard-boiled, peeled
- 1 cup shredded parmesan cheese, low-fat

Method:

1. Switch on the air fryer, insert fryer basket, grease it with olive oil, then shut with its lid, set the fryer at 400 degrees F, and preheat for 10 minutes.
2. Meanwhile, place all the ingredients except for eggs, mustard and cheese in a bowl, mix gently and then shape the mixture into four patties.
3. Place an egg in the center of each patty, then shape it around the egg and coat with parmesan cheese, pressing the cheese into the meat.
4. Open the fryer, add eggs in it, spray with olive oil, close with its lid and cook for 15 minutes until nicely golden and cooked, turning the eggs halfway through.
5. When air fryer beeps, open its lid, transfer eggs onto a serving plate and serve with mustard.

Nutrition Value:

- Calories: 533 Cal
- Fat: 43 g
- Carbs: 2 g
- Protein: 33 g
- Fiber: 1 g

Steak Nuggets

Preparation time: 40 minutes
Cooking time: 15 minutes
Servings: 4

Ingredients:

- 1 pound beef steak, cut into chunks
- 1 large egg

For Breading:

- 1/2 teaspoon seasoned salt
- 1/2 cup pork panko
- 1/2 cup grated parmesan cheese

For Chipotle Ranch Dip:

- 1/4 of a medium lime, juiced
- 1/2 teaspoon ranch dressing and dip mix
- 1 teaspoon chipotle paste
- 1/4 cup mayonnaise
- 1/4 cup sour cream

Method:

1. Prepare the ranch dip and for this, place all its ingredients in a bowl and whisk well until mixed; reserve its 1 teaspoon and refrigerate until required.
2. Prepare breading and for this, place all its ingredients in a shallow dish and stir until mixed.
3. Crack the egg in a bowl and then whisk well until blended.
4. Prepare nuggets and for this, dip steak pieces into the egg, then dredge into the breading until coated, arrange them on a sheet pan lined with baking paper and freeze for 30 minutes.
5. Then switch on the air fryer, insert fryer basket, grease it with olive oil, then shut with its lid, set the fryer at 325 degrees F, and preheat for 5 minutes.
6. Open the fryer, add steak nuggets in it in a single layer, spray with olive oil, close with its lid and cook for 3 minutes until nicely golden and cooked.

7. When air fryer beeps, open its lid, transfer nuggets onto a serving plate, keep warm and cook remaining nuggets in the same manner.
8. Serve nuggets with ranch dip.

Nutrition Value:

- Calories: 350 Cal
- Fat: 20 g
- Carbs: 1 g
- Protein: 40 g
- Fiber: 0 g

Beef and Mushroom Patties

Preparation time: 10 minutes
Cooking time: 20 minutes
Servings: 5

Ingredients:

- 1 pound ground beef
- 6 medium mushrooms
- 1 teaspoon onion powder
- 1/2 teaspoon salt
- 1 teaspoon garlic powder
- 1/2 teaspoon ground black pepper
- 1 tablespoon Maggi seasoning sauce

Method:

1. Switch on the air fryer, insert fryer basket, grease it with olive oil, then shut with its lid, set the fryer at 320 degrees F, and preheat for 10 minutes.
2. Meanwhile, rinse mushrooms, drain them well, add them in a food processor and then pulse until puree.
3. Then add remaining ingredients except for ground beef and pulse for 1 minute until smooth.
4. Tip the mushroom mixture in a bowl, add turkey, stir well and then shape the mixture into five patties.
5. Open the fryer, add patties in it in a single layer, spray with olive oil, close with its lid and cook for 10 minutes until nicely golden and cook through, shaking the basket every 5 minutes and flipping the patties halfway through.
6. When air fryer beeps, open its lid, transfer patties onto a serving plate, and serve.

Nutrition Value:

- Calories: 221.4 Cal
- Fat: 8.3 g
- Carbs: 11.1 g
- Protein: 26.4 g
- Fiber: 2.5 g

Italian-Style Meatballs

Preparation time: 15 minutes
Cooking time: 25 minutes
Servings: 4

Ingredients:

- 2/3 pound ground beef
- 2 tablespoons minced shallots
- 1/3 pound turkey sausage
- 1 tablespoon minced garlic
- 1/4 cup chopped parsley
- 1 tablespoon Dijon mustard
- 1/2 teaspoon salt
- 1 tablespoon chopped thyme
- 1 tablespoon chopped rosemary
- 2 tablespoons olive oil
- 1 egg, beaten
- 1/4 cup whole-wheat panko crumbs
- 2 tablespoons almond milk
- Zucchini noodles for serving

Method:

1. Place panko crumbs in a bowl, add milk, stir and let it stand for 5 minutes.
2. Meanwhile, take a skillet pan, place it over medium-high heat, add oil and when hot, add shallots and cook for 2 minutes until softened.
3. Then add minced garlic, cook for 1 minute until fragrant, and then remove the pan from heat.
4. Add shallot mixture in a large bowl, pour in milk mixture along with sausage, beef, salt, thyme, rosemary, mustard, and parsley and stir until combined.
5. Switch on the air fryer, insert fryer basket, grease it with olive oil, then shut with its lid, set the fryer at 400 degrees F, and preheat for 5 minutes.
6. Meanwhile, prepare meatballs and for this, shape the beef mixture into 1 ½ inch meatballs.

7. Open the fryer, add meatballs in it in a single layer, spray them with olive oil, close with its lid and cook for 10 minutes until nicely golden and cooked through, shaking the basket every 5 minutes and turning meatballs halfway through.
8. When air fryer beeps, open its lid, transfer meatballs onto a serving plate, keep them warm and cook remaining meatballs in the same manner.
9. Serve meatballs with zucchini noodles.

Nutrition Value:

- Calories: 122 Cal
- Fat: 8 g
- Carbs: 0 g
- Protein: 10 g
- Fiber: 0 g

Rib Eye Steak

Preparation time: 10 minutes
Cooking time: 17 minutes
Servings: 1

Ingredients:

- 16 ounces rib-eye steak, about 1 ½-inch thick
- 1/2 teaspoon garlic powder
- 1 teaspoon salt
- 3/4 teaspoon ground black pepper
- 3/4 teaspoon steak seasoning

Method:

1. Switch on the air fryer, insert fryer basket, grease it with olive oil, then shut with its lid, set the fryer at 350 degrees F, and preheat for 5 minutes.
2. Meanwhile, stir together garlic powder, salt, black pepper, and steak seasoning and then sprinkle it on all sides of steak.
3. Open the fryer, add steak in it, spray with olive oil, close with its lid, and cook for 12 minutes until nicely golden and thoroughly cooked, turning and spraying with olive oil halfway through.
4. When air fryer beeps, open its lid, transfer steak onto a serving plate, cover it with foil, and let it rest for 10 minutes, then cut it into slices and serve.

Nutrition Value:

- Calories: 230 Cal
- Fat: 16 g
- Carbs: 0 g
- Protein: 21 g
- Fiber: 0 g

Steak Bites and Mushrooms

Preparation time: 5 minutes
Cooking time: 23 minutes
Servings: 4

Ingredients:

- 1 pound steaks, 1-inch cubed
- 8 ounces mushrooms, halved
- ¼ teaspoon ground black pepper
- 1/2 teaspoon garlic powder
- ¾ teaspoon salt
- 1 teaspoon Worcestershire sauce
- 2 tablespoons unsalted butter, melted
- 1 tablespoon minced parsley

Method:

1. Switch on the air fryer, insert fryer basket, grease it with olive oil, then shut with its lid, set the fryer at 400 degrees F, and preheat for 5 minutes.
2. Meanwhile, place steak cubes in a bowl, add mushrooms and stir until just mixed.
3. Drizzle with butter, season with garlic powder, black pepper, salt, and Worcestershire sauce and toss until well coated.
4. Open the fryer, add steaks and mushrooms in it, spread them evenly, close with its lid, and cook for 18 minutes until nicely golden and cooked, shaking and the basket and turning steaks every 5 minutes.
5. When air fryer beeps, open its lid, transfer steaks and mushrooms onto a serving plate and serve.

Nutrition Value:

- Calories: 330 Cal
- Fat: 21 g
- Carbs: 3 g
- Protein: 32 g
- Fiber: 1 g

Pork Chops

Preparation time: 10 minutes
Cooking time: 28 minutes
Servings: 4

Ingredients:

- 4 pork chops, bone-in
- 1 teaspoon onion powder
- 1 teaspoon garlic powder
- 1/8 teaspoon allspice
- 1 teaspoon dried parsley
- 1 teaspoon paprika
- 2 cups crushed pork rinds

Method:

1. Switch on the air fryer, insert fryer basket, grease it with olive oil, then shut with its lid, set the fryer at 400 degrees F, and preheat for 10 minutes.
2. Meanwhile, prepare pork chops, and for this, brush them with olive oil on both sides until coated.
3. Place the remaining ingredients in a small bowl and then dredge pork chops in it until evenly coated.
4. Open the fryer, add pork chops in it, close with its lid and cook for 18 minutes until nicely golden and crispy, shaking the basket every 5 minutes, flipping the pork chops halfway through.
5. When air fryer beeps, open its lid, transfer pork chops onto a serving plate and serve.

Nutrition Value:

- Calories: 371 Cal
- Fat: 20 g
- Carbs: 1 g
- Protein: 44 g
- Fiber: 1 g

Pork Dumplings with Dipping Sauce

Preparation time: 10 minutes
Cooking time: 52 minutes
Servings: 4

Ingredients:

- 4 ounces ground pork
- 4 cups chopped bok choy
- 1 teaspoon olive oil
- 1 tablespoon grated ginger
- 1 tablespoon minced garlic
- 1/4 teaspoon crushed red pepper
- 18 dumpling wrappers, about 3 1/2-inch square

For the Dip:

- 1 tablespoon chopped scallions
- 1/2 teaspoon coconut sugar
- 2 tablespoons apple cider vinegar
- 2 teaspoons soy sauce
- 1 teaspoon toasted sesame oil

Method:

1. Take a skillet pan, place it over medium-high heat, add oil and when hot, add bok choy, stir and cook for 6 to 8 minutes until wilted.
2. Then stir in garlic and ginger, cook for 1 minute until fragrant, then remove the pan from heat, let bok choy cool for 5 minutes and then pat dry with paper towels.
3. Spoon bok choy mixture in a bowl, add ground pork and crushed red pepper and stir until well combined.
4. Prepare the dumplings and for this, place a dumpling wrapper on clean working space, place 1 tablespoon of pork mixture in the center, then brush water on the edges, and then fold it over the filling to make half-moon shape dumpling.
5. Press the edges of wrap to seal the dumplings, place it on a plate, and prepare remaining dumplings in the same manner.
6. Switch on the air fryer, insert fryer basket, grease it with olive oil, then shut with its lid, set the fryer at 375 degrees F, and preheat for 5 minutes.

7. Open the fryer, add dumplings in it in a single layer, spray with oil, close with its lid and cook for 12 minutes until nicely golden brown and cooked, shaking the basket every 5 minutes and turning the dumpling halfway.
8. In the meantime, prepare the dip and for this, place all its ingredients in a bowl and whisk until combined.
9. When air fryer beeps, open its lid, transfer dumplings onto a serving plate, keep warm and cook remaining dumplings in the same manner.

Nutrition Value:

- Calories: 140 Cal
- Fat: 5 g
- Carbs: 16 g
- Protein: 7 g
- Fiber: 1 g

Spicy Bacon Bites

Preparation time: 5 minutes
Cooking time: 15 minutes
Servings: 2

Ingredients:

- 4 strips of bacon
- 1/2 cup crushed pork rinds
- 1/4 cup hot sauce

Method:

1. Switch on the air fryer, insert fryer basket, grease it with olive oil, then shut with its lid, set the fryer at 350 degrees F, and preheat for 5 minutes.
2. Meanwhile, cut bacon into six pieces, place them in a bowl, drizzle with hot sauce, then toss until coated and dredge with pork rinds.
3. Open the fryer, add bacon pieces in it, spray with olive oil, close with its lid and cook for 10 minutes until nicely golden and crispy, shaking the basket every 5 minutes.
4. When air fryer beeps, open its lid, transfer bacon onto a serving plate and serve.

Nutrition Value:

- Calories: 120.7 Cal
- Fat: 8.7 g
- Carbs: 0 g
- Protein: 7.3 g
- Fiber: 0 g

Spicy Lamb Steak

Preparation time: 40 minutes
Cooking time: 35 minutes
Servings: 4

Ingredients:

- 1 pound lamb sirloin steaks, boneless
- 4 slices of ginger
- 1/2 of a white onion
- 5 cloves of garlic, peeled
- 1 teaspoon ground fennel
- 1 teaspoon salt
- 1/2 teaspoon ground cardamom
- 1 teaspoon cayenne pepper
- 1 teaspoon garam masala
- 1 teaspoon ground cinnamon

Method:

1. Place all the ingredients in a blender, except for lamb, and pulse for 4 minutes until blended.
2. Place lamb chops in a bowl, make cuts in it with a knife, add marinade, toss until well coated and marinate for a minimum for 30 minutes.
3. Then switch on the air fryer, insert fryer basket, grease it with olive oil, then shut with its lid, set the fryer at 330 degrees F, and preheat for 5 minutes.
4. Open the fryer, add lamb steaks in it in a single layer, spray them with oil, close with its lid and cook for 15 minutes until nicely golden and cooked through, shaking the basket every 5 minutes, flipping halfway through.
5. When air fryer beeps, open its lid, transfer lamb steaks onto a serving plate, keep it warm and cook remaining steaks in the same manner.
6. Serve straight away.

Nutrition Value:

- Calories: 182 Cal
- Fat: 7 g
- Carbs: 3 g
- Protein: 24 g
- Fiber: 1 g

Herbed Lamb Chops

Preparation time: 5 minutes
Cooking time: 22 minutes
Servings: 4

Ingredients:

- 1 pound lamb chops
- 1 teaspoon salt
- 1 teaspoon dried oregano
- 1 teaspoon dried rosemary
- 1 teaspoon coriander
- 1 teaspoon dried thyme
- 2 tablespoons lemon juice
- 2 tablespoons olive oil

Method:

1. Place all the ingredients except for lamb in a large plastic bag, seal the bag, and shake until well mixed.
2. Add lamb chops into the plastic bag, seal the bag, shake until well coated and marinate in the refrigerator for a minimum of 1 hour.
3. Then switch on the air fryer, insert fryer basket, grease it with olive oil, then shut with its lid, set the fryer at 390 degrees F, and preheat for 5 minutes.
4. Then open the fryer, add lamb chops in it in a single layer, spray with olive oil, close with its lid and cook for 8 minutes until nicely golden and cooked through, shaking the basket every 5 minutes, flipping lamb chops halfway through.
5. When air fryer beeps, open its lid, transfer lamb chops onto a serving plate, keep them warm and cook remaining lamb chops in the same manner.
6. Serve straight away.

Nutrition Value:

- Calories: 280 Cal
- Fat: 12.3 g
- Carbs: 8.3 g
- Protein: 32.7 g
- Fiber: 1.2 g

Chapter 10: Vegetarian

Brussels Sprouts

Preparation time: 10 minutes
Cooking time: 14 minutes
Servings: 4

Ingredients:

- 2 cups Brussels sprouts, cut into quarters
- 1/4 teaspoon sea salt
- 1 tablespoon olive oil

Method:

1. Switch on the air fryer, insert fryer basket, grease it with olive oil, then shut with its lid, set the fryer at 375 degrees F, and preheat for 5 minutes.
2. Meanwhile, place Brussel sprouts in a large bowl, drizzle with oil, and then season with salt and toss until well coated.
3. Open the fryer, add sprouts in it, close with its lid and cook for 9 minutes until nicely golden and crispy, shaking the basket every 5 minutes.
4. When air fryer beeps, open its lid, transfer sprouts onto a serving plate, and serve.

Nutrition Value:

- Calories: 50 Cal
- Fat: 4 g
- Carbs: 4 g
- Protein: 1 g
- Fiber: 2 g

Roasted Rainbow Vegetables

Preparation time: 5 minutes
Cooking time: 25 minutes
Servings: 4

Ingredients:

- 1 medium red bell pepper, deseeded, 1-inch cubed
- 4 ounces mushrooms, halved
- 1 medium yellow summer squash, deseeded, 1-inch cubed
- 1/2 of sweet onion, peeled, cut into 1-inch wedges
- 1 medium zucchini, 1-inch cubed
- ½ teaspoon salt
- ½ teaspoon ground black pepper
- 1 tablespoon olive oil

Method:

1. Switch on the air fryer, insert fryer basket, grease it with olive oil, then shut with its lid, set the fryer at 350 degrees F, and preheat for 5 minutes.
2. Meanwhile, place all the ingredients in a large bowl and toss until well coated.
3. Open the fryer, add vegetables in it in an even layer, close with its lid and cook for 20 minutes until nicely golden and crispy, shaking the basket every 5 minutes, stirring halfway through.
4. When air fryer beeps, open its lid, transfer vegetables onto a serving plate and serve.

Nutrition Value:

- Calories: 69 Cal
- Fat: 3.8 g
- Carbs: 7.7 g
- Protein: 2.6 g
- Fiber: 2.3 g

Falafel

Preparation time: 1 hour and 10 minutes
Cooking time: 35 minutes
Servings: 4

Ingredients:

For Falafels:

- 1 cup dried chickpeas, soaked overnight
- 3 tablespoons almond flour
- ¼ cup cilantro leaves
- 1 medium red onion, peeled, chopped
- 1 teaspoon minced garlic
- 3/4 teaspoon ground cumin
- 1/2 teaspoon baking powder
- 1/4 allspice
- 1 teaspoon ground coriander
- 3/4 teaspoon salt
- 2 tablespoons olive oil

For Tahini Yoghurt Sauce:

- 1 teaspoon tahini paste
- 1 lemon, juiced
- 1 tablespoon olive oil
- 1 cup Greek yogurt

Method:

1. Prepare yogurt sauce and for this, place all its ingredients in a bowl, whisk until well combined, and set aside until required.
2. Prepare falafels, and for this, place chickpeas in a food processor, add onion, garlic, and cilantro and pulse until ground.
3. Slowly blend in oil until incorporated, then tip the mixture in a bowl, add remaining ingredients, mix well and refrigerate for 1 hour.
4. Then switch on the air fryer, insert fryer basket, grease it with olive oil, then shut with its lid, set the fryer at 370 degrees F, and preheat for 5 minutes.

5. Meanwhile, prepare falafel balls and for this, roll falafel mixture into balls, 2 tablespoons of mixture per ball.
6. Open the fryer, add falafel balls in it in a single layer, spray with oil, close with its lid and cook for 15 minutes until nicely golden, crispy, and cooked through, shaking the basket halfway through.
7. When air fryer beeps, open its lid, transfer falafel onto a serving plate, cover with aluminum foil and cook remaining falafel balls in the same manner.
8. Serve falafel balls with prepared yogurt sauce.

Nutrition Value:

- Calories: 366 Cal
- Fat: 18 g
- Carbs: 40 g
- Protein: 15 g
- Fiber: 10 g

Green Beans with Bacon

Preparation time: 5 minutes
Cooking time: 25 minutes
Servings: 4

Ingredients:

- 3 slices of bacon, diced
- 1 teaspoon ground black pepper
- 3 cups cut green beans
- 1 teaspoon salt
- 1/4 cup water

Method:

1. Switch on the air fryer, insert fryer basket, then shut with its lid, set the fryer at 375 degrees F, and preheat for 5 minutes.
2. Meanwhile, take a baking pan that fits into the air fryer, add bacon, onion, and green beans in it, pour in water, and stir until just mixed.
3. Then open the fryer, add baking pan in it, close with its lid, cook for 15 minutes, stirring the beans halfway through.
4. Then season beans and bacon with salt, stir well, set the fryer temperature to 400 degrees F, and continue cooking for 5 minutes.
5. When air fryer beeps, open its lid, take out the pan, cover it, and then let green beans and bacon rest for 5 minutes.
6. Serve straight away.

Nutrition Value:

- Calories: 95 Cal
- Fat: 6 g
- Carbs: 6 g
- Protein: 3 g
- Fiber: 2 g

Parmesan Brussel Sprouts

Preparation time: 10 minutes
Cooking time: 30 minutes
Servings: 8

Ingredients:

- 24 ounces Brussel sprouts, fresh
- ¼ cup sliced almonds
- 1 teaspoon salt
- 2 tablespoons coconut oil
- 2 tablespoons bagel seasoning
- ¼ cup grated parmesan cheese
- 2 cups of water

Method:

1. Take a saucepan, place it over medium heat, add sprouts, pour in water, and cook for 10 minutes.
2. Then drain the sprouts, let them cool for 5 minutes, slice sprouts in half and place them in a bowl.
3. Switch on the air fryer, insert fryer basket, grease it with olive oil, then shut with its lid, set the fryer at 220 degrees F, and preheat for 5 minutes.
4. Meanwhile, add remaining ingredients into the sprouts and then toss until well combined.
5. Open the fryer, add sprouts in it, spray with olive oil, close with its lid and cook for 15 minutes until nicely golden and crispy, shaking the basket every 5 minutes.
6. When air fryer beeps, open its lid, transfer sprouts onto a serving plate, and serve.

Nutrition Value:

- Calories: 75 Cal
- Fat: 4 g
- Carbs: 8 g
- Protein: 4 g
- Fiber: 3 g

Ginger Soy Tofu

Preparation time: 15 minutes
Cooking time: 60 minutes
Servings: 4

Ingredients:

For Tofu:

- 14 ounces tofu, pressed, drained
- 1 teaspoon garlic powder
- 1/2 teaspoon smoked paprika
- 1/4 cup arrowroot flour
- 1 teaspoon salt
- 1/2 teaspoon ground cumin

For Gingery Soy Sauce:

- 1 teaspoon garlic powder
- 2 tablespoons agave nectar
- 1 tablespoon grated ginger
- 1/4 teaspoon ground black pepper
- 3 tablespoons soy sauce
- 1 tablespoon coconut oil
- 2 tablespoons coconut sugar
- 1 teaspoon white sesame seeds
- 1 scallion, chopped

Method:

1. Switch on the air fryer, insert fryer basket, grease it with olive oil, then shut with its lid, set the fryer at 350 degrees F, and preheat for 10 minutes.
2. Meanwhile, cut tofu in slices, cut each slice into eight squares, and place tofu pieces in a plastic bag.
3. Add remaining ingredients, seal the bag, and shake well until well coated.
4. Open the fryer, add tofu pieces in it in a single layer, spray with olive oil, close with its lid and cook for 25 minutes until nicely golden and crispy, shaking the basket every 5 minutes and turning halfway through.

5. Meanwhile, prepare the sauce and for this, place all its ingredients in a large bowl except for sesame seeds and scallion and whisk until combined, set aside until required.
6. When air fryer beeps, open its lid, transfer tofu pieces to plate, keep them warm, and cook remaining tofu pieces in the same manner.
7. When done, transfer tofu pieces to the bowl containing prepared sauce and toss until coated.
8. Garnish tofu with sesame seeds and scallion and then serve.

Nutrition Value:

- Calories: 139 Cal
- Fat: 4.4 g
- Carbs: 17.8 g
- Protein: 10.3 g
- Fiber: 1.6 g

Loaded Potatoes

Preparation time: 10 minutes
Cooking time: 30 minutes
Servings: 4

Ingredients:

- 11 ounces baby potatoes
- 2 slices of bacon, center-cut
- 1 1/2 tablespoons chopped chives
- 1/8 teaspoon salt
- 1 teaspoon olive oil
- 2 tablespoons shredded Cheddar cheese
- 2 tablespoons sour cream

Method:

1. Switch on the air fryer, insert fryer basket, grease it with olive oil, then shut with its lid, set the fryer at 350 degrees F, and preheat for 5 minutes.
2. Meanwhile, place potatoes in a bowl, drizzle with oil and toss until coated.
3. Open the fryer, add potatoes in it, close with its lid and cook for 25 minutes until nicely golden, crispy and fork-tender, shaking the basket every 5 minutes and turning potatoes halfway through.
4. In the meantime, take a skillet pan, place it over medium heat, add bacon, cook for 7 minutes or until crispy, then transfer it to a cutting board and crumble it.
5. When air fryer beeps, open its lid, transfer potatoes onto a serving plate, lightly crush them and then drizzle with bacon dripping.
6. Season potatoes with salt, top with sour cream and chives, sprinkle with chives and bacon, and serve.

Nutrition Value:

- Calories: 199 Cal
- Fat: 7 g
- Carbs: 26 g
- Protein: 7 g
- Fiber: 4 g

Veggie Quesadillas

Preparation time: 10 minutes
Cooking time: 25 minutes
Servings: 4

Ingredients:

- 1 cup sliced red bell pepper
- 1 cup cooked black beans
- 1 cup sliced zucchini
- 1/4 teaspoon ground cumin
- 1 teaspoon lime zest
- 1 tablespoon lime juice
- 2 tablespoons chopped cilantro
- 1 cup shredded cheddar cheese
- 2 ounces Greek yogurt
- 1/2 cup drained pico de gallo
- 4 whole-wheat flour tortillas, each about 6-inch

Method:

1. Prepare quesadilla and for this, place tortilla wraps on working space, sprinkle 2 tablespoons of cheddar over half of each wrap, top cheese with ¼ cup each of black beans, zucchini, and red pepper, and then top with remaining cheese.
2. Cover filling with the other half of tortillas, making a moon-shaped quesadilla, then secure with a toothpick and spray with oil.
3. Switch on the air fryer, insert fryer basket, grease it with olive oil, then shut with its lid, set the fryer at 400 degrees F, and preheat for 5 minutes.
4. Open the fryer, add quesadilla in it in a single layer, close with its lid and cook for 10 minutes until nicely golden, crispy, and vegetables have softened, turning quesadilla halfway through.
5. When air fryer beeps, open its lid, transfer quesadilla onto a serving plate, keep it warm and cook remaining quesadilla in the same manner.
6. Serve straight away.

Nutrition Value:

- Calories: 291 Cal

- Fat: 8 g
- Carbs: 36 g
- Protein: 17 g
- Fiber: 8 g

Chapter 11: Fish and Seafood

Tomato Basil Scallops

Preparation time: 10 minutes
Cooking time: 20 minutes
Servings: 2

Ingredients:

- 8 jumbo sea scallops
- 12 ounces frozen spinach, thawed, drained
- 1 tablespoon chopped basil
- 1 tablespoon tomato paste
- 1 teaspoon minced garlic
- 1/2 teaspoon salt and more as needed
- 1/2 teaspoon ground black pepper and more as needed
- 2 tablespoons olive oil
- 3/4 cup heavy whipping cream

Method:

1. Switch on the air fryer, then shut with its lid, set the fryer at 350 degrees F, and preheat for 10 minutes.
2. Meanwhile, take an air fryer baking pan and then line spinach evenly in the bottom.
3. Place scallops in a bowl, drizzle with oil, season with salt and black pepper, toss until coated, and then top them over spinach.
4. Place tomato paste in a bowl, add garlic, basil, ¼ teaspoon each of salt and black pepper, and cream, whisk until mixed and then spread the mixture over scallops.
5. Open the fryer, insert baking pan in it, close with its lid and cook for 10 minutes until thoroughly cooked and sauce is bubbling.
6. When air fryer beeps, open its lid, take out the baking pan, transfer spinach and scallops onto a serving plate and serve.

Nutrition Value:

- Calories: 359 Cal

- Fat: 33 g
- Carbs: 6 g
- Protein: 9 g
- Fiber: 2 g

Fish Sticks

Preparation time: 10 minutes
Cooking time: 25 minutes
Servings: 4

Ingredients:

- 1 pound cod fillets
- 1 1/2 cups pork rind panko
- 2 tablespoons Dijon mustard
- ½ teaspoon ground black pepper
- 2/3 teaspoon salt
- ¾ teaspoon Cajun seasoning
- 2 tablespoons water
- 1/4 cup mayonnaise

Method:

1. Prepare fish sticks and for this, pat dry cod fillets, then cut them into 1 by 2 inches wide sticks and set aside until required.
2. Place mayonnaise in a bowl, add water and mustard and whisk until combined.
3. Place pork rinds in a shallow dish, add Cajun seasoning, season with salt and black pepper and stir until mixed.
4. First, dip each fish stick into the mayonnaise mixture, then dredge with pork rind mixture, place it on a plate, and coat remaining fish sticks in the same manner.
5. Switch on the air fryer, insert fryer basket, grease it with olive oil, then shut with its lid, set the fryer at 400 degrees F, and preheat for 5 minutes.
6. Open the fryer, add fish sticks in it in a single layer, spray with olive oil, close with its lid and cook for 10 minutes until nicely golden and crispy, shaking the basket every 5 minutes and filling the fish sticks halfway through.
7. When air fryer beeps, open its lid, transfer fish sticks onto a serving plate, keep them warm and cook remaining fish sticks in the same manner.
8. Serve straight away.

Nutrition Value:

- Calories: 263 Cal
- Fat: 16 g
- Carbs: 1 g
- Protein: 26.4 g
- Fiber: 0.5 g

Salmon Patties

Preparation time: 5 minutes
Cooking time: 7 minutes
Servings: 2

Ingredients:

- 8 ounces fresh salmon fillet, deboned
- 1 lemon, sliced
- 1/4 teaspoon garlic powder
- 1/8 teaspoon salt
- 1 egg

Method:

1. Switch on the air fryer, insert fryer basket, grease it with olive oil, then shut with its lid, set the fryer at 390 degrees F, and preheat for 5 minutes.
2. Meanwhile, cut salmon into bite-size pieces, add them into the food processor, add remaining ingredients, and then process until incorporated.
3. Tip the salmon mixture in a bowl and then shape it into four patties.
4. Open the fryer, add salmon patties in it, spray them with olive oil, close with its lid and cook for 7 minutes until nicely golden and crispy, turning the patties halfway through.
5. When air fryer beeps, open its lid, transfer salmon patties onto a serving plate and serve.

Nutrition Value:

- Calories: 250.4 Cal
- Fat: 11.4 g
- Carbs: 2.3 g
- Protein: 32.3 g
- Fiber: 0.2 g

Shrimp Scampi

Preparation time: 10 minutes
Cooking time: 7 minutes
Servings: 4

Ingredients:

- 25 shrimps, defrosted, peeled, deveined, cleaned
- 1 tablespoon minced garlic
- 1 teaspoon dried basil
- 2 teaspoons red pepper flakes
- 1 teaspoon dried chives
- 4 tablespoons unsalted butter
- 1 tablespoon lemon juice
- 2 tablespoons chicken stock

Method:

1. Switch on the air fryer, insert fryer baking pan, grease it with olive oil, then shut with its lid, set the fryer at 330 degrees F, and preheat for 5 minutes.
2. Open the fryer, add garlic, red pepper, and butter in it, close with its lid and cook for 2 minutes until the butter has melted.
3. Then add remaining ingredients into the baking pan, stir gently, shut the air fryer with lid and continue cooking for 5 minutes until shrimps have cooked through.
4. When air fryer beeps, open its lid, take out the baking pan and let shrimps rest for 1 minute.
5. Stir the shrimps, transfer them to a plate and serve.

Nutrition Value:

- Calories: 221 Cal
- Fat: 13 g
- Carbs: 1 g
- Protein: 23 g
- Fiber: 0 g

Garlic Lime Shrimp

Preparation time: 10 minutes
Cooking time: 8 minutes
Servings: 2

Ingredients:

- 1 cup fresh shrimps, peeled, deveined, cleaned
- ½ teaspoon minced garlic
- 1/8 teaspoon ground black pepper
- 1 lime, juiced
- 1/8 teaspoon salt
- 5 wooden skewers, each about 6-inch, soaked

Method:

1. Switch on the air fryer, insert fryer basket, grease it with olive oil, then shut with its lid, set the fryer at 220 degrees F, and preheat for 10 minutes.
2. Meanwhile, place shrimps in a bowl, season with salt and black pepper, add garlic and lime juice, toss until well mixed and then thread them onto the skewers.
3. Open the fryer, add shrimps in it in a single layer, close with its lid and cook for 8 minutes until nicely golden and cooked through, turning shrimps halfway through.
4. When air fryer beeps, open its lid, transfer shrimps onto a serving plate, and serve.

Nutrition Value:

- Calories: 76 Cal
- Fat: 1 g
- Carbs: 4 g
- Protein: 13 g
- Fiber: 0 g

Parmesan Shrimp

Preparation time: 5 minutes
Cooking time: 25 minutes
Servings: 4

Ingredients:

- 2 pounds jumbo shrimp, peeled, deveined, cooked
- 2 teaspoons minced garlic
- 1/2 teaspoon dried oregano
- 1 teaspoon ground black pepper
- 1 teaspoon dried basil
- 1 teaspoon onion powder
- 2/3 cup grated parmesan cheese
- 2 tablespoons olive oil
- 1 lemon, quartered

Method:

1. Switch on the air fryer, insert fryer basket, grease it with olive oil, then shut with its lid, set the fryer at 350 degrees F, and preheat for 5 minutes.
2. Meanwhile, place all the ingredients in a bowl and toss until well mixed and coated.
3. Open the fryer, add shrimps in it in a single layer, close with its lid and cook for 10 minutes until nicely golden brown and cooked through, turning shrimps halfway through.
4. When air fryer beeps, open its lid, transfer shrimps onto a serving plate, keep them warm and cook remaining shrimps in the same manner.
5. Serve straight away.

Nutrition Value:

- Calories: 30.7.7 Cal
- Fat: 16.4 g
- Carbs: 12.2 g
- Protein: 27.6 g
- Fiber: 3 g

Salmon and Asparagus

Preparation time: 10 minutes
Cooking time: 18 minutes
Servings: 2

Ingredients:

- 2 salmon fillets, deboned, each about 6 ounces
- 2 tablespoons dill
- 1 bunch of asparagus
- 2 tablespoons chopped parsley
- ½ teaspoon salt
- ½ teaspoon ground black pepper
- 1 tablespoon olive oil
- 1 1/2 tablespoons lemon juice

Method:

1. Switch on the air fryer, insert fryer basket, grease it with olive oil, then shut with its lid, set the fryer at 400 degrees F, and preheat for 10 minutes.
2. Meanwhile, place lemon juice and olive oil, add salt, black pepper, parsley, and dill and stir until mixed.
3. Prepare salmon, and for this, coat the leash of each fillet with ¾ of parsley mixture.
4. Place asparagus in another bowl, add reserved parsley mixture, and toss until combined.
5. Open the fryer, spread asparagus in the bottom, top with salmon, spray with olive oil, close with its lid and cook for 8 minutes until nicely golden and cooked through, turning salmon halfway through.
6. When air fryer beeps, open its lid, transfer salmon and asparagus onto a serving plate and serve.

Nutrition Value:

- Calories: 391 Cal
- Fat: 19 g
- Carbs: 9 g
- Protein: 48 g
- Fiber: 5 g

Catfish with Green Beans

Preparation time: 10 minutes
Cooking time: 25 minutes
Servings: 2

Ingredients:

- 2 catfish fillets, each about 6-ounces
- 12 ounces fresh green beans, trimmed
- 3/8 teaspoon salt, divided
- 1/4 teaspoon ground black pepper
- 1/2 teaspoon crushed red pepper
- 1 1/2 teaspoon chopped dill
- 1 teaspoon swerve sweetener
- 1/8 teaspoon coconut sugar
- 1/4 cup almond flour
- 1/3 cup panko breadcrumbs
- 2 tablespoons olive oil
- 1/2 teaspoon apple cider vinegar
- 1 egg, beaten
- 3/4 teaspoon dill pickle relish
- 2 tablespoons mayonnaise
- Lemon wedges for serving

Method:

1. Switch on the air fryer, insert fryer basket, grease it with olive oil, then shut with its lid, set the fryer at 400 degrees F, and preheat for 5 minutes.
2. Meanwhile, take a medium bowl, add green beans in it, drizzle with oil, season with 1/8 teaspoon salt, red pepper, and sweetener and toss until coated.
3. Open the fryer, add green beans in it, close with its lid and cook for 12 minutes until nicely golden brown and tender, shaking the basket every 5 minutes.
4. In the meantime, dredge fish fillets with almond flour, then dip in beaten egg and coat with panko bread crumbs, pressing them lightly into the fillets.
5. When air fryer beeps, open its lid, transfer green beans onto a serving plate, wrap with foil to keep them warm, and set aside until required.

6. Add prepared fillets into the fryer basket, spray them with olive oil, and continue cooking for 8 minutes until nicely golden brown and thoroughly cooked.
7. Prepare dip and for this, place mayonnaise in a bowl, add sugar, dill, vinegar, and relish and stir until mixed.
8. When done, season fillets with remaining salt and black pepper and serve with green beans, prepared dip and lemon wedges.

Nutrition Value:

- Calories: 416 Cal
- Fat: 18 g
- Carbs: 31 g
- Protein: 33 g
- Fiber: 12 g

Chapter 12: Dessert

Apple Chips

Preparation time: 5 minutes
Cooking time: 15 minutes
Servings: 6

Ingredients:

- 6 large red apples
- 1/8 teaspoon ground cinnamon
- 1 teaspoon olive oil

Method:

1. Switch on the air fryer, insert fryer basket, grease it with olive oil, then shut with its lid, set the fryer at 350 degrees F, and preheat for 5 minutes.
2. Meanwhile, place core each apple, cut into wedges, then place them in a bowl, drizzle with oil and toss until coated.
3. Open the fryer, add apple wedges in it, close with its lid and cook for 10 minutes until nicely golden and crispy, shaking the basket every 5 minutes.
4. When air fryer beeps, open its lid, transfer apple chips onto a serving plate, sprinkle with cinnamon, and serve.

Nutrition Value:

- Calories: 608 Cal
- Fat: 6 g
- Carbs: 150 g
- Protein: 2 g
- Fiber: 26 g

Churros

Preparation time: 1 hour and 15 minutes
Cooking time: 35 minutes
Servings: 4

Ingredients:

- 1/3 cup unsalted butter
- 1 cup almond flour
- 1/2 cup coconut sugar
- 2 tablespoons erythritol sweetener
- 1/4 teaspoon salt
- 3/4 teaspoon ground cinnamon
- 1 teaspoon vanilla extract, unsweetened
- 2 eggs
- 1 cup of water

Method:

1. Cut butter into cubes, place it into a saucepan, then place it over medium-high heat, add salt, sweetener, and water and bring the mixture to boil.
2. Switch heat to medium-low level, add flour and stir it continuously until a smooth dough comes together.
3. Remove pan from heat, then transfer the dough to a bowl and let cool for 5 minutes.
4. Add eggs and vanilla, mix with an electric mixture until dough comes together, and then transfer the dough into a large piping bag with a star-shaped tip.
5. Take a baking sheet, grease it with olive oil, then pipe churros on it, about 4-inch long and cutting the ends with a scissor, and then refrigerate for 1 hour.
6. Then switch on the air fryer, insert fryer basket, grease it with olive oil, then shut with its lid, set the fryer at 375 degrees F, and preheat for 5 minutes.
7. Open the fryer, add churros in it in a single layer, ½-inch apart, spray with olive oil, close with its lid, and cook for 12 minutes until nicely golden, shaking the basket every 5 minutes.
8. Meanwhile, place coconut sugar in a large bowl, add cinnamon in it, stir until mixed and set aside until required.

9. When air fryer beeps, open its lid, transfer churros into the bowl containing cinnamon-sugar mixture, toss until coated, and cook remaining churros in the same manner.
10. Serve straight away.

Nutrition Value:

- Calories: 442.5 Cal
- Fat: 31 g
- Carbs: 33.2 g
- Protein: 9 g
- Fiber: 3.3 g

Fruit Crumble Mug Cakes

Preparation time: 5 minutes
Cooking time: 20 minutes
Servings: 4

Ingredients:

- 1 small peach, cored, diced
- 4 plums, pitted, diced
- 2 tablespoons oats
- 1 small apple, cored, diced
- 4 ounces almond flour
- 1 small pear, diced
- 2 tablespoons swerve caster sugar
- 1 ¾ tablespoon coconut sugar
- 1 tablespoon honey
- 2 ounces unsalted butter
- ¼ cup blueberries, diced

Method:

1. Switch on the air fryer, insert fryer basket, grease it with olive oil, then shut with its lid, set the fryer at 320 degrees F, and preheat for 5 minutes.
2. Meanwhile, take four heatproof mugs or ramekins, evenly fill them with fruits, and then cover with coconut sugar and honey.
3. Place flour in a bowl, add butter and caster sugar, then rub with fingers until the mixture resembled crumbs, then stir in oats and evenly spoon this mixture into prepared fruit mugs.
4. Open the fryer, place fruit mugs in it, close with its lid, cook for 10 minutes, then increase air fryer temperature to 390 degrees F and continue cooking for 5 minutes until the top have nicely browned and crunchy.
5. When air fryer beeps, open its lid, carefully take out the mugs and serve straight away.

Nutrition Value:

- Calories: 380 Cal
- Fat: 11 g
- Carbs: 68 g
- Protein: 5 g
- Fiber: 5 g

Banana Bread

Preparation time: 10 minutes
Cooking time: 45 minutes
Servings: 4

Ingredients:

- 3/4 cup whole wheat flour
- 3/4 cup mashed bananas
- 1/2 teaspoon salt
- 1 teaspoon cinnamon
- 2 tablespoons toasted walnuts, chopped
- 1/2 cup coconut sugar
- 1/4 teaspoon baking soda
- 1 teaspoon vanilla extract, unsweetened
- 2 tablespoons olive oil
- 1/3 cup Greek yogurt
- 2 eggs, beaten

Method:

1. Switch on the air fryer, insert fryer basket, then shut with its lid, set the fryer at 310 degrees F, and preheat for 10 minutes.
2. Meanwhile, take a 6-inch round cake pan, line it with parchment paper, spray with olive oil and set aside until required.
3. Place flour in a bowl, add salt, cinnamon, and baking soda and stir until mixed.
4. Crack eggs in another bowl, add mashed banana, coconut sugar, vanilla, yogurt, and oil and whisk well until incorporated.
5. Slowly whisk egg-banana mixture into the flour mixture until well combined, and smooth batter comes together, then spoon the batter into the prepared cake pan and top with walnuts.
6. Open the fryer, place cake pan in it, close with its lid, and cook for 30 to 35 minutes until top is nicely golden and the cake has thoroughly cooked.
7. When air fryer beeps, open its lid, take out the cake pan, then transfer cake to the wire rack and cool for 15 minutes.
8. Cut cake into slices and serve.

Nutrition Value:

- Calories: 180 Cal
- Fat: 6 g
- Carbs: 29 g
- Protein: 4 g
- Fiber: 2 g

Cheesecake Bites

Preparation time: 40 minutes
Cooking time: 12 minutes
Servings: 2

Ingredients:

- 1/2 cup almond flour
- 1/2 cup and 2 tablespoons erythritol sweetener
- 1/2 teaspoon vanilla extract, unsweetened
- 8 ounces cream cheese, softened
- 4 tablespoons heavy cream, divided

Method:

1. Place softened cream cheese in the bowl of a stand mixer, add 2 tablespoons of cream and ½ cup sweetener and mix until blended and smooth.
2. Take a baking sheet, line it with a baking sheet, place cream cheese mixture on it, spread evenly, and place it into the freezer for a minimum of 30 minutes until firm.
3. Then switch on the air fryer, insert fryer basket, grease it with olive oil, then shut with its lid, set the fryer at 300 degrees F, and preheat for 5 minutes.
4. Meanwhile, place almond flour in a shallow dish, add remaining sweetener and stir until mixed.
5. Cut frozen cheesecake into bite-size pieces, then dip into remaining heavy cream and dredge with almond flour mixture until well coated.
6. Open the fryer, add cheesecake bites in it in a single layer, close with its lid and cook for 2 minutes until nicely golden and crispy.
7. When air fryer beeps, open its lid, transfer cheesecake bites onto a serving plate and cook remaining cheese bites in the same manner.
8. Serve straight away.

Nutrition Value:

- Calories: 329.3 Cal
- Fat: 30.7 g
- Carbs: 6.6 g
- Protein: 6.6 g
- Fiber: 1.5 g

Spiced Apples

Preparation time: 5 minutes
Cooking time: 12 minutes
Servings: 4

Ingredients:

- 4 small apples, cored, sliced
- 1 teaspoon apple pie spice
- 2 tablespoons coconut sugar
- 2 tablespoons coconut oil, melted
- 4 tablespoons whipped topping

Method:

1. Switch on the air fryer, insert baking basket, grease it with olive oil, then shut with its lid, set the fryer at 350 degrees F, and preheat for 5 minutes.
2. Meanwhile, place apple slices in a bowl, drizzle with oil, sprinkle with sugar and apple pie spice and toss until well coated.
3. Open the fryer, add apple pieces in the baking pan, close with its lid and cook for 12 minutes until tender, shaking the basket every 5 minutes.
4. When air fryer beeps, open its lid, take out the baking pan, transfer apple to a serving plate, top with whipped topping, and serve.

Nutrition Value:

- Calories: 233 Cal
- Fat: 10.6 g
- Carbs: 32.6 g
- Protein: 1.7 g
- Fiber: 3.6 g

Key Lime Cupcakes

Preparation time: 20 minutes
Cooking time: 25 minutes
Servings: 6

Ingredients:

- 2 limes, juiced, zested
- 1 teaspoon vanilla extract, unsweetened
- ¼ cup swerve caster sugar
- 8 ounces Greek yogurt
- 2 eggs
- 1 egg yolk
- 7 ounces cream cheese, softened

Method:

1. Place yogurt in a bowl, add cream cheese and mix with a hand mixer until creamy.
2. Then whisk in eggs, egg yolk, lime juice, lime zest, and vanilla until incorporated and then evenly divide the mixture between six silicone muffin cups, reserving the rest of the batter for later use.
3. Switch on the air fryer, insert fryer basket, grease it with olive oil, then shut with its lid, set the fryer at 320 degrees F, and preheat for 5 minutes.
4. Open the fryer, stack muffin cups in it, close with its lid, cook for 10 minutes and then continue cooking for 10 minutes at 350 degrees F until thoroughly cooked.
5. When air fryer beeps, open its lid, transfer muffins to a wire rack, and let cool for 10 minutes.
6. Then place reserved batter in a piping bag, then pipe the batter onto the cupcake and refrigerate them for 4 hours until the top has set.
7. Serve straight away.

Nutrition Value:

- Calories: 218 Cal
- Fat: 14 g
- Carbs: 13 g
- Protein: 9 g
- Fiber: 0 g

Grilled Pineapple

Preparation time: 10 minutes
Cooking time: 28 minutes
Servings: 4

Ingredients:

- 1 medium pineapple, peeled, cored
- 2 teaspoons ground cinnamon
- 1/2 cup coconut sugar
- 3 tablespoons melted unsalted butter

Method:

1. Switch on the air fryer, insert fryer basket, grease it with olive oil, then shut with its lid, set the fryer at 400 degrees F, and preheat for 10 minutes.
2. Meanwhile, place sugar in a bowl, add cinnamon, and stir until mixed.
3. Cut pineapple into spears, brush them generously with melted butter, and then coat them with the sugar-cinnamon mixture, pressing lightly.
4. Open the fryer, add pineapple in it in a single layer, close with its lid and cook for 10 minutes until nicely golden and crispy, shaking the basket every 5 minutes and brushing with melted butter halfway through.
5. When air fryer beeps, open its lid, transfer pineapple pieces onto a serving plate, keep them warm and cook remaining pineapple for 8 minutes.
6. Serve straight away.

Nutrition Value:

- Calories: 295 Cal
- Fat: 8 g
- Carbs: 57 g
- Protein: 1 g
- Fiber: 3 g

Conclusion

The Mediterranean diet has been one of the best diets and for good reasons. The meal plan consists of heart-healthy foods that use fresh produce, whole grains, and healthy fats for contributing to better heart health, weight loss and reduce risks of other diseases.

If you are thinking of trying out the Mediterranean diet, an amazing kitchen tool can help you a lot in maintaining your healthy eating routine. Say hello to the air fryer. It's a modern tool that cooks all the foods without the fat and turns out more healthy meals with great taste.

In short, with the Mediterranean diet and air fryer, you will never feel dieting, and you can carry it out entire life.

Printed in Great Britain
by Amazon

36700653R00064